MARK W. ERWIN

THE
POWERS

12 PRINCIPLES TO
TRANSFORM YOUR LIFE
FROM ORDINARY TO
EXTRAORDINARY

Skyhorse Publishing

Skyhorse Publishing books may be purchased in bulk at special discounts for sales promotion, corporate gifts, fund-raising, or educational purposes. Special editions can also be created to specifications. For details, contact the Special Sales Department, Skyhorse Publishing, 307 West 36th Street, 11th Floor, New York, NY 10018 or info@skyhorsepublishing.com.

Skyhorse® and Skyhorse Publishing® are registered trademarks of Skyhorse Publishing, Inc.®, a Delaware corporation.

Visit our website at www.skyhorsepublishing.com.

10 9 8 7 6 5 4 3 2 1

Library of Congress Cataloging-in-Publication Data is available on file.

Cover design by Rain Saukas
Cover photo credit: iStock

ISBN: 978-1-5107-0616-3
Ebook ISBN: 978-1-5107-0617-0

Printed in the United States of America

"It is not in the stars to hold our destiny but in ourselves."
—William Shakespeare (1564–1616)

To my grandchildren: Della, Lila, Virginia, and my new grandson, Thomas Erwin Highsmith.

To the heroes, mentors, and friends discovered along my path to success.

To those who desire exceptional success and are willing to make the personal changes necessary to achieve it.

Table of Contents

Preface

In my experience, success comes to those who let themselves dream of possibilities. Through perseverance, they overcome obstacles and achieve far beyond their dreams. We all fall down at times, but success is about learning from our mistakes and endeavoring to not repeat our failures.

This book is for the very few who are driven to be exceptional—the small number willing to do the hard work to achieve a remarkable life of success and fulfillment. You might even say these people are on a quest. If you set your course for a life of incredible success, no matter what the field, *The Powers* will provide you with lessons that can help you on your journey.

It's never too early or too late to begin striving for success. History is full of examples of people who have moved from an ordinary life to one of extraordinary success. While it is human nature to desire the respect and acceptance of others, some people are also driven by an intense desire to make a difference and to succeed, while others are driven by a deep-seated fear of failure. Either of these extremes can ignite your passion.

In his book *Human Accomplishment*, Charles Murray says, "Human beings have been most magnificently productive and reach their highest peaks in the times and places where humans have thought most deeply about their place in the universe and been most convinced they have one."[1]

My friend Mike Gaddis says, in his wonderful book *Legend's Legacy*, "Pursue life with a passion. Put everything you have into it. Never settle for less than yourself. There is too much to see and feel. One lifetime won't be enough."[2]

This book is built around a simple premise that has had a profound impact on my own quest for success: each of us, no matter our field of work, level of education, race, gender, persuasion, or creed, possesses a set of Powers that, when properly harnessed and put to work, will bring great achievement. We live in a storytelling culture so I have included many stories of other exceptional people. Throughout this book, you will find valuable principles that have lasted long after their authors passed into history. This wisdom lives on because it represents the highly refined, pressed down, and distilled essence of truth.

I have read many books about success, and I have many friends who are successful. I will share the great knowledge I've acquired from these experiences in *The Powers*.

Conventional wisdom says that by age seventy-one I should be retired to a life of relaxation and contemplation. Since my whole life has been unconventional, it seems to me my assignment now is to leave something behind that might help others. This volume is my legacy to those who might need encouragement along their own path to their destiny. I hope you will find the Powers I have discovered useful on your personal journey. In reading this book you will be inspired to discover what is possible in your life, to set lofty goals, and to develop the skills you need to meet— and far exceed—them.

Do you have a vision for your future? Do you want to know how to go from an observer of life to an influencer, and a doer on grander stages than you could have possibly imagined?

If you answered yes to either of these questions, this is the book for you. There are a few things worth mentioning as you start your journey. First, if you're expecting an authoritative guide to living your life exactly how I tell you, then you will be disappointed. I will not tell you what to do. What I am interested in is helping you understand the Powers you possess that will enable you to achieve your dreams and goals, whatever they are. Second, if you have picked up this book and are reading it, then you are precisely who it is written for. Congratulations on taking the first step toward success!

While everyone has different goals and dreams, and that's a wonderful thing, every person reading this book possesses the same set of Powers, even if some of them are hidden deep inside you.

Different folks have different strengths and weaknesses. Some people find it easy to retain knowledge, but difficult to establish and focus on goals. Others are powerful vision-casters, but struggle to persist. What I want to communicate to you is that while all of the Powers outlined in this book are important, none are static or stationary. Much like the human brain itself, these Powers are dynamic and elastic. You can work at and improve upon any and all of them, no matter where you've been or where you are in life.

In the chapters ahead, I will explain both what these Powers are and what they look like in practical application, and I will show you how to discover and cultivate your strongest Powers and grow those other Powers you struggle with.

I will share my encounters, mistakes, and wisdom from a lifetime of experiential learning. In the chapters ahead, you will read about many of my triumphs, but you will also read about more than a few of my failures. It may seem counterintuitive to dwell on failure in a book about success, but anyone who has achieved success knows the importance of failure.

Steve Jobs, in a commencement address at Stanford University, spoke truthfully about the nature of failure when he said,

I didn't see it then, but it turned out that getting fired from Apple was the best thing that could have ever happened to me. The heaviness of being successful was replaced by the lightness of being a beginner again, less sure about everything. It freed me to enter one of the most creative periods of my life.

During the next five years, I started a company named NeXT, another company named Pixar, and fell in love with an amazing woman who would become my wife. Pixar went on to create the world's first computer-animated feature film, Toy Story, and is now the most successful animation studio in the world. In a remarkable turn of events, Apple bought NeXT, I returned to Apple, and the technology we developed at NeXT is at the heart of Apple's current renaissance. . . .

I'm pretty sure none of this would have happened if I hadn't been fired from Apple. It was awful-tasting medicine, but I guess the patient needed it. Sometimes life hits you in the head with a brick. Don't lose faith. I'm convinced that the only thing that kept me going was that I loved what I did. You've got to find what you love. And that is as true for your work as it is for your lovers. Your work is going to fill a large part of your life, and the only way to be truly satisfied is to do what you believe is great work. And the only way to do great work is to love what you do. If you haven't found it yet, keep looking. Don't settle. As with all matters of the heart, you'll know when you find it. And, like any great relationship, it just gets better and better as the years roll on. So keep looking until you find it. Don't settle.[3]

If you get one thing from this book, I hope it is a deeper understanding of, and appreciation for, the sentiment that lies at the core of Jobs's story: You can overcome or surpass almost any obstacle. It doesn't matter where you've been or where you are now. All that matters is where you're going.

Success isn't an easy thing to attain. Each of these Powers takes hard work and discipline, but I firmly believe that by cultivating the Powers in your own life, it is possible for each and every one of you to attain your goals, whatever they are.

So turn the page, and let's start making our dreams a reality, together.

Make a Difference—Do Good—Have Fun—and
Never Retire

In the Beginning

"Every adversity, every failure, every heartache carries with it the seed of an equal or greater benefit."

—Napoleon Hill

Unlike most rags-to-riches tales, mine is a riches-to-rags, and then back to more meaningful riches story.

I was born into a family of wealth and privilege. Our ancestors go back to the founding days of America. Sandwich, the first town to be established on Cape Cod in Massachusetts, was founded in 1637 by the persuasive and energetic Edmund Freeman, of whom I am a descendant. While my family history is a bit murky in places since those early days, I do know that my family was also deeply involved in the Revolutionary War.

Edmund Freeman's descendant, my grandfather, Charles Hughes Freeman, and his partner, William C. Yawkey, were the first oil barons of West Virginia, forming a solid success foundation for the Freeman family. Yawkey, who originally hired my grandfather as his lawyer, was a successful timber baron who was reportedly the wealthiest man in the state of Michigan at the beginning of the twentieth century. He asked my grandfather to travel to West Virginia to assess the value of land he had been offered as payment for a debt owed by a partner in another venture.

Grandfather and Yawkey's son Bill rode the train together to Charleston, West Virginia, and then hired a wagon to take a look at the property. While they were exploring the land, Grandfather was intrigued when he observed a mountain spring that was on fire. When he discovered that the fire was caused by oil and natural gas leaking from the ground, he was surprised that the extensive and valuable fossil fuel resources had not been developed by anyone. Seeing the opportunity of a lifetime, my grandfather reported back to Yawkey and proposed a partnership to acquire and develop additional land to help take advantage of the original holdings, forming Yawkey and Freeman Coal Co. They hit their first oil gusher in 1906 and went on to tap more than 350 successful wells in the early twentieth century, eventually selling their business to South Penn Oil Co., which later became Pennzoil Corp. Their foresight and entrepreneurial spirit resulted in tremendous wealth and privilege for my grandfather and his family. When Grandfather married my grandmother in 1910, newspapers reported he was worth an estimated ten million dollars.

A newspaper account of his death in 1920 quoted a friend of my grandfather's, calling him "one of the warm-est-hearted men I have ever known." His friend said, "He was a man of sympathetic insight and charitable judgment, a loyal friend and a citizen of the first order." I strive to live up to his great legacy even today.

Due to the Great Depression and years of excess by those in the family's next generation, my grandfather's fortune didn't survive far into my generation. Perhaps this was fortunate for me. Had the wealth been passed on, I may never have been inspired to develop my own skills, ambition, and Grand Vision to restore our family reputation and fortune. His daughter, my mother, Joan, was a free-spirited socialite who was used to getting whatever she desired, including three husbands. As a child, I witnessed her decline into depression, alcoholism, and despair. Our home life was sad and gloomy.

By my teenage years, I was becoming restless and rebellious. I had been smoking since I was nine and drank fairly regularly at about twelve—coincidentally the same year I spent my first night in jail.

My sixteen-year-old half-brother, his friends, and I were driving around, drinking Country Club Malt Liquor and throwing the empty cans at the school building when the police caught us. One guy ran and got away, but the rest of us were caught and taken to the police station. The policeman took me aside because of my young age and said, "Just tell us the name of the 'rabbit' that got away, and we will let you go home." I said, "I'm no rat," so I spent the night with the others.

By the tenth grade, I had developed such a poor attitude that I skipped most of the school year and was expelled. The principal of the school said, "Son, you have plenty of potential, but until you decide to use it, we do not have a place for you."

At the time of my expulsion, because of my mother's poor judgment and excessive pleasures, little wealth remained. Mother was forced to take a job as a sales clerk in a women's shop to make ends meet.

Since my grandfather had been one of the early owners of the Detroit Tigers, I like to say I was born on third base, but then the family struck out. I felt like my mother had squandered my heritage on fast living and bad decisions. Resentment and disappointment led to anger and rebellion. I began to hang out with people who shared my defiant spirit. I never gave a thought to the future. My future rested in the next moment of anger. My behavior was predictable and would lead to disaster sooner than expected.

My friends and I were constantly in trouble with the law. Among many other criminal activities, I developed a scheme I thought was foolproof and undetectable. I wrote checks for small amounts and forged Mother's signature. Since she was never quite sober, how could I get caught?

Well, it turns out Mother paid closer attention to her finances than I thought. In March 1961, at age sixteen, the police arrested me for check fraud, and I was put in juvenile hall to await trial.

I felt alone, powerless, and vulnerable. It was the first time I realized that I had absolutely no control over anything in my life. But this rock-bottom moment would become a turning point for me.

One frightening night, while in my cell, I reached out to God for the first time in my life and told Him I was ashamed and afraid. When I asked for forgiveness and mercy, I felt something inexplicable and indefinable. I knew He had responded to my plea for mercy with love and grace. How I knew, I cannot explain—but I knew He was holding me. I told Him, with His help, I would try to be someone He could be proud of in heaven.

Then, days later, a kindly judge gave me a second chance by giving me a choice of serving four years in prison or joining the military for the same term. The decision was easy. I had no financial resources and little education, so my prospects were few.

Through that judge, God had answered my prayer and given me a way out of my predicament. I did not know at the time that the judge had done so much more for me. He had put me on a path of discovery.

When I joined the Air Force, I had no self-discipline and no self-respect, both of which are key traits for successfully navigating life. If there's one thing the Air Force taught me, it was that if I did what they told me to do, when they told me to do it, I would be fine. If I didn't, I would be punished immediately.

The concept of doing what I was told, when I was told to do it, was not one that I absorbed immediately. During basic training, I attempted to defy the rules, but I didn't get very far. We recruits were to be given a weekend pass to leave the base after four weeks of training, but I decided to leave with some other recruits a week early. I was caught coming back on base on the floor of a car. The sergeant said, "Erwin, you are not even worth the [gun] powder to blow you up." He made me do a hundred push-ups, assigned me extra guard duty, and deferred my first promotion. I was learning fast that wisdom usually comes from experience, and that many times the most valuable experiences are the hard, difficult, and challenging experiences. I paid for that bad decision, but the lesson was entirely worth it. The Air Force made it clear that they were not kidding—they would treat me fairly, but they were also going to hold me to my word. They proved that they were in charge, which allowed me to quit worrying about asserting my own freedom and develop some discipline. This experience proved what I have since discovered over and over again: To be a leader, you must first be willing to be lead yourself. To possess self-discipline is to possess the highest form of self-knowledge, and it is ultimately this self-knowledge that will guide you on the path to success.

Most important, you are the only person in charge of your future.

One of the biggest benefits of learning discipline is developing self-control, or the ability to self-regulate, even under extraordinary circumstances and pressures.

One of the other key lessons I had to learn early was that the Air Force would not always be there for me to impose discipline and order whenever I came up short. I needed to learn how to do what is supposed to be done even when no one else is looking. It's easy to do the right thing when you have superiors or peers watching you constantly, but the real challenge is continuing to have the discipline to act (or not act, in many cases) when no one will know whether or not you did the right thing.

So how do you accomplish this? We all have two inner voices, one of which is emotional and impulsive or compulsive, and another that is a more reasoned and rational voice. Recognize both for what they are and you can be anybody you want to be. You must develop your reasoned inner voice; it tells you when you're doing the wrong or right thing and inspires you to stay on course when the going gets tough. It's important to cultivate an inner voice that can drown out the compulsive and impulsive voice competing for attention. This can also be referred to as thinking for yourself, which is one of the common denominators among successful people.

Most of us are born into a society where social and political infrastructures, also called mores, are already established for us. Whether or not we want to admit it, this is a form of control. The design of our homes, the clothing we wear, the music we listen to, even the entertainment we subscribe to, has a tendency to do our thinking for us. We go along with what has been established for us without question, while anyone going against it is considered antiestablishment or even rebellious.

In our individual roles within the larger society, many of us refuse to do certain things that are not in keeping with the latest of everything. For example, many wouldn't wear clothing that's not in style. But "in style" only means that someone else is dictating what you should wear. In style means wearing the same styles—the result being that you will blend in and not be unique.

The media is used as a means of conditioning us with biased information. Ads are created to move us to act in ways that are beneficial to the businesses that seek our economic support. Without even realizing it, you can begin to live a life that others have designed for you, which makes it difficult for you to understand your own dreams and goals, let alone pursue them. This information put out for us is called propaganda. During wars, each side tries to affect the attitudes of the enemy by the use of propaganda. This same negative connotation is now called advertising.

I believe that the Internet has created untold potential and is enabling truly remarkable developments, but we must be wary of our tendency to allow ourselves to be told what do to, what to buy, and how to live through this invasive, persistent source of endless information. In order for you to become exceptional you must decide how you can be authentic. You won't need to rebel against everything presented to you but you do need to interpret and decide what is really important to you.

So what are the characteristics of someone who thinks for himself or herself? First, you will make decisions based on your own observations and judgments, instead of accepting the opinion of someone else. This means thinking rationally about problems, something I'll talk about in more detail later, but ultimately, it means being able to entertain an idea without embracing it, as Aristotle once said. Thinking for yourself also means that you take the time to carefully evaluate a situation and, if it seems reasonable, take a stand and eventually show that you can accept responsibility for your own decisions, good or bad.

Becoming an independent thinker certainly has its perks, the first and most important of which is that you will learn to trust yourself and your ability to make sound decisions. That will come in handy in pursuing your goals to fulfillment. Independent thinkers also gain the ability to stand up for what they believe and lose the irrational fear of being unique. Independent thinkers also have a greater sense of freedom, which broadens their view of life and adds more dimension and opportunity for self-development. They tend to be more aware of what the media is trying to sell them, which plays back into the ability to think rationally about their choices and decisions.

Cultivating the ability to think for yourself doesn't come in handy just when making business, political, or financial decisions. Sometimes, personal and family decisions will require an even greater commitment to this principle. Self-awareness is the essential first step toward maximizing your potential. Self-awareness can improve your judgment and help you identify opportunities for personal growth. Each of us is born with unique personality traits and God-given talents. Self-awareness is having a clear perception of your own personality and recognizing your particular talents as well as limitations. This knowledge lets you manage your inner world. That in turn helps you deal with your weaknesses and maximize your strengths.

You cannot succeed without first realizing your own potential and deciding to put it to work. From there, it becomes a matter of developing a vision to inspire you when everything seems to conspire to overwhelm your days.

One great example of the importance of knowing yourself comes from the early days of my relationship with my wife of many years, Joan.

Before I dated her, I had another girlfriend whom I brought home to meet my mother. At that time, my mother was living on the old family estate, which had become over-grown, run-down, and a little abandoned. Despite my initial trepidation, Mother really liked this girl a lot. Not only did they have a shared love of adventure and a daring lifestyle, their greatest common denominator was a flighty attitude, which they both possessed in spades. They had a grand time laughing and conversing with each other, bouncing around conversational topics—ranging from art to religion to the weather.

Fortunately for me, that relationship didn't work out, and later, I was able to take Joan home to meet my mother. This time, the introduction didn't go nearly as well. Joan and my mother did not hit it off at all. Mother relayed to me her opinion that the other girl was a much more open-minded, free spirit. She even went so far as to predict that if I married Joan, our marriage would not last more than five years.

On the drive home from West Virginia, I decided that the best course of action would be to pray for wisdom and guidance in making a decision about my future with Joan. It hit me at some point in the drive that I needed to trust myself, rather than the input of a woman who had been in three failed marriages and endured many years of unhap-piness. While I loved my mother dearly, I realized that she likely never experienced the wonderful benefits of eternal, unconditional love.

It was after that realization that I prayed to God to allow me to spend the rest of my life with Joan, because I knew that she was the soul mate I needed to guide and inspire me on my journey through life.

After receiving her father's permission and blessing to ask Joan to marry me, I proposed two weeks before Easter in 1968. I was caught completely off guard when she stunned me with a less than enthusiastic response. She said, "I love you, but I'm not sure I'm ready to be married. I'll need two weeks to think about it before I can give you an answer. During that time, I don't want to see you."

Needless to say, it was an anxious couple of weeks. Despite the constant worry and with the hope that she would ultimately say yes, we continued to speak on the phone every day, and I continued to pray fervently that the Lord would intervene and convince Joan that I was the right man for her, and that our marriage would be what the Lord wanted for both of us. I was certainly convinced that was true, but it was stressful waiting for her to reach that same conclusion.

At the end of the two weeks, I went to her house for Easter lunch, nervous but more than ready to hear her final response. I would be lying if I said that I wasn't afraid she was going to tell me she wasn't ready. Fortunately for me, when I showed up at her house for lunch, I was greeted with all the enthusiasm and joy I could have possibly asked for. Joan gave me a gift of my favorite aftershave and then gave me the answer I had been hoping and praying for a long time to hear: yes.

We were married in Maryville, Tennessee, in August 1968, and two years later, I received this letter from my mother:

Dearest Top,

I just wanted to let you know how pleased I am with the progress you have made in the process of growing up. Joan and marriage have been very good for you; I do hope you have been good for her.

I don't think you know, or realize, that God has given you the gift of saying just the right things to make people feel better. Don't ever abuse it with dishonesty. I am very pleased with the change in you.

Lovingly,

Mother

That letter was a tremendous validation for me, despite our initial disagreements about whether or not Joan was the right soul mate for me. Perhaps, most important, I learned a crucial lesson about the importance of developing a loud inner voice that allows you to drown out the other voices competing for your attention.

If I had not been able to develop that watchful and reasoned inner voice, perhaps I would have listened to my mother and taken her opinion more seriously, and I would have missed out on one of the best things ever to happen to me.

suc•cess
(sək-ses') *n.*
1. The achievement
of something
desired.

The Power of You

*"5 percent of the people think; 10 percent of the people think
they think; and the other 85 percent would rather die than
think."*

—Thomas Edison

I t is said that in life we all strive to move from survival
to stability, to success, then to significance and, finally,
to legacy. What do you want most? Is it financial independence, fame, exceptional talent, admiration, respect, power,
happiness? Success is whatever you decide it is for you.

Seeking success is a personal quest. Therefore, you
will be making the most critical decision of your life. But
remember, being successful doesn't define you as much as
it reveals who and what you're capable of becoming. This
is called self-actualization, and represents "everything that

one is capable of becoming." Self-actualization becomes the fulfillment of the possibilities of one's character and personality. Success is a relative term, and as my friend, famed artist Bob Timberlake, says, "Success is not finding the pot of gold at the end of the rainbow as much as it is about the journey along the way."

I've known many remarkably successful people. They've succeeded in every field, including art, sports, sales, business, education, politics, writing, acting, religion, and more. These people come in all types, sizes, and shapes. I've learned that success has been achieved not just by the smartest or cleverest, nor is it confined to the most talented, best looking, or the most popular. A great example is George Shinn, an author, self-made millionaire, and founding owner of an NBA franchise. George grew up in a small mill town in the South. His father died when he was eight, and his mother worked several jobs to survive. In the fifth grade, Shinn endured humiliation when a classmate announced that little George was so poor he was receiving free school lunches. George said, "From that point on, I decided that I would never be embarrassed [by poverty] again, and that I would follow every principle and all the right rules to get ahead and succeed."

Shinn struggled through high school. He was never a good student but he made a promise to his mother to graduate and kept it. He graduated last in his class of 232 students. After reading Dr. Norman Vincent Peale's *The Power of Positive Thinking*, he applied the principles he learned and developed a stronger belief in himself.

Shinn credited his mother with teaching him her own idea of the Triangle of Success:

I have seen many other triangles of success but none quite like hers. She said, "On one side is health; take care of yourself because if you are not healthy, everything else becomes secondary. On the other side is positive attitude. You have to have a positive attitude about yourself and your dreams. The foundation of the triangle is faith. You have to have faith, primarily in God, but also in yourself and others."[4]

Shinn had a passion to be somebody. He went to work in a textile mill and began working part time as a janitor to pay his way through a small business college. He became a recruiter for the school and was such a great salesman that by age twenty-three he was running the school and later became a partner. As Vietnam veterans came back to

America, enrollment in private business schools increased dramatically. He began acquiring other privately owned schools, ultimately building a chain of thirty, which he named Rutledge Education System.

In 1987, Shinn decided Charlotte, North Carolina, was a large enough market to secure a NBA basketball franchise. He convinced a major bank to back him and began preparing an application. George and I were having lunch with the CEO of the bank just before the submission deadline. During our conversation I told Shinn I was pretty sure Charlotte could win one of the new expansion teams based on a recent demographic/sociographic study I had conducted on the region for my development business. He turned to me and said, "What is a demographic/sociographic study?" When I explained, he said, "Can you share your study with me so I can add it to my application?" I did, and he later gave me four of the best seats in the new arena.

George became successful, not because he was smart or well-connected but because he had a wise mother whom he loved and listened to. He also had an early vision, "to never be embarrassed again." Fear of failure drove him as much as wanting to make his mother proud.

Successful people lead themselves first, and then those around them. As the master of your destiny, you are the only one who can chart your course. You, too, can achieve whatever you decide is important enough for you to pursue passionately.

Know Your Real Potential

If you are a normal, reasonably well-balanced person with average or better intelligence, of any race, nationality, size, shape, or other persuasion, you have unrealized potential. If you have not inventoried your personal gifts and limitations, now is the time to do a bit of introspection. Most of us aren't inclined to spend much time on self-reflection, especially those with low self-esteem. Even when personal feedback is presented to us, we're not always open to it, since honest feedback isn't always flattering. But you must be strong and persist to overcome this fear.

Whenever you are tempted to avoid honest introspection or feedback from those who know you well, remember that self-knowledge, or self-realization, is key to success. Knowing your strengths and your weaknesses, where your talents lie and where you could use discipline, allows you to live in the sphere of who you really are. Putting yourself in situations that utilize your gifts and talents will lead to a far more fulfilling existence than struggling through life attempting to succeed in places where you may be limited.

I know many of my limitations, but it has taken a lifetime to understand some of them. For example, I have always struggled with rote memorization of facts and dates. I really struggled with trying to learn a second language though I have friends who excel in multiple languages. My brain simply isn't wired for that kind of learning. On the other hand,

I am a rational and logical thinker, a self-learner, and am highly persistent.

Early on, without the knowledge of my abilities and limitations, I didn't care how long someone tried to teach me a language, for instance, because I was convinced I wasn't any good at learning to begin with. Of course, this made me feel intellectually inferior to others, but what I had to realize was that others possess thinking patterns that made them better at skills like rote memorization.

If you are one of those people who have gone through life feeling inferior, I would encourage you to remember that everyone is different. No two people possess the same set of strengths and weaknesses. Just because you can't do things other people can, doesn't mean you are not intelligent and won't be as successful. An example I like to give is that there are plenty of doctors and surgeons who are brilliant medical professionals. They typically have a gift of easy memorization of data, languages, and facts, but many are completely useless at managing and balancing a checkbook.

Another great example of this kind of self-knowledge is a partner and friend of mine for many years, John Crosland. He grew up with all of the privileges that come with a financially successful family and attended the best schools. Unfortunately, he was highly dyslectic, suffering from a learning disability involving difficulties in acquiring and processing language that is typically exhibited by a lack of proficiency in reading, spelling, and writing. As a result, he struggled with school his whole young life. It wasn't until later in his life that his learning disability was diagnosed as dyslexia.

When John graduated from a prestigious college his classmates selected him as "Most Likely to Fail." His family agreed. What everyone underestimated about John was his gigantic gift of dogged persistence and a drive to prove them all wrong. He spent his career out-working everybody around him. In order to learn he would write on notepads whatever he heard and then study them until he felt he fully understood. He almost never accepted no for an answer. He would just keep coming back with a different argument until he got what he wanted. John Crosland became my mentor and business partner and I am a witness that he by far exceeded every expectation of him all his life. John once said to me, "If you try hard enough, you can overcome anything."

Similarly, knowing that my strong suits were conceptual, logical, rational thinking, as well as persistence, and that my biggest weakness was fact and data memorization, didn't mean that I couldn't be successful. It only meant that I had to know myself well enough to adapt according to the gifts I had been given. While in college I was searching for a subject for a homework assignment in English composition, and I said to my grandmother, who was well into her eighties, "I need a great quotation to build a five-page composition for my English class. Do you have any you can recommend?"

"Bring me a piece of paper," she replied. From memory, she wrote out the following quotation by President Calvin Coolidge and told me to memorize it and write my composition. It read, "Nothing in the world can take the place of persistence. Talent will not; nothing is more common than unsuccessful men with talent. Genius will not; unrewarded genius is almost a proverb. Education will not; the world is full of educated derelicts. Persistence and determination alone are omnipotent."

I could not memorize the quotation but have lived by this concept since the day I first read it. Getting to know your potential takes boldness and courage but is more than worth it in the long run.

Find the place where your gifts and your passions collide and begin to build your life up from there into the fulfilling life you always imagined. When I found that place, I was able to achieve far beyond what anyone, including me, thought I could when I was seventeen years old.

The particular strengths I possess are less important to my success than knowing what they are and playing into them. The Power, after all, is not being one type of learner versus another type. Self-awareness helps you find situations in which you will be most effective and helps with intuitive decision-making.

The Real 1 Percent Rule

Many years ago, someone shared with me the teachings of an Indian philosopher who suggested that, within any given group of people—whether it's a company, city, committee, or a family—a tiny percentage of the people (say, 1 percent) will make change happen. These people are called "Doers." A bit larger group (say, 9 percent) will watch what is happening and are called "Observers."

The remainder of the population simply doesn't know and/or doesn't care, for a variety of reasons, ranging from having never reached stability in their lives, to being so entitled by support from other sources they become self-involved. This includes those who have received inheritances as well as those who receive government support due to poverty. Call these the DK/DC (don't know/don't care).

Those individuals in the DK/DC category (which is most of the world, for better or worse) are constantly in survival or sustainability mode, either by circumstance or choice. Some are worried about where the next meal or job is going to come from.

Others are in a sustainable state of existence, but simply don't care about the larger world around them. These people are satisfied with who they are and have no ambition to be anything more than that. They can also tend to be so self-absorbed that they have actively decided not to care about anything else.

When *Newsweek* recently asked one thousand US citizens to take America's official citizenship test, 29 percent couldn't name the vice president of the United States. Seventy-three percent couldn't correctly say why we fought the Cold War. Forty-four percent were unable to define the Bill of Rights. And 6 percent couldn't even circle Independence Day on a calendar.

In a recent international "Ignorance Survey," nearly twelve thousand Americans were questioned, and our nation placed second-highest (topped only by Italy) in lacking a basic understanding of some of the most fundamental aspects of our society.[5]

Perhaps worse, ABC reported the results of a joint survey with *Newsweek* that found "many Americans remain surprisingly ignorant of the [Constitution's] provisions." The survey went on to find that "61 percent didn't know that the length of a US senator's term is six years, 63 percent couldn't name the number of Supreme Court justices on the bench (nine), and 86 percent didn't know that 435 members fill the US House of Representatives. . . . Few could recite the opening phrase of the Constitution ('We the people of the United States') or list the constitutional requirements to be president (natural born, at least thirty-five years old, and permanent resident of the United States)."[6] This obvious disinterest in current events and the fundamental tenets of

American society are perfect examples of the DK/DC attitude toward life.

Those few who are natural Doers, however, are people who have an indefatigable drive to *accomplish*. Doers don't sit and watch; they look at a situation, company, or challenge and commit to changing whatever needs to be changed to make it better. Personally, I've always been one of those people who stands up and says, "I want to make a difference." Sometimes, all it takes is the courage to raise your hand to change the world.

I know by experience that the Indian philosopher's observation that only a tiny 1 percent will make a change is correct. Over the years, I've refined the theory further to understand that each of us has within ourselves all three elements: Doer, Observer, and DK/DC. By way of example, I'm an observer when it comes to football and most other sports. In the art of opera, I'm clearly a DK/DC, as I don't have a clue and just don't care. In my pursuit of success, I needed to become a Doer in finance.

It's worth noting the paradox of being a Doer: you have to take risks to be a Doer, and you have to be a Doer to take risks. Take Michael Jordan, for instance, one of my favorite athletes.

It's not a mystery why Michael Jordan became such a Doer. In high school he played baseball, football, and basketball, so he had athletic ability but was unfocused. When he tried out for the varsity basketball team during his sophomore year, he did not make the cut. This failure seems to have lit a motivational fire to prove his worth. So Jordan became the star of the junior varsity squad. That summer he focused his attention on basketball and drove himself constantly. His junior year he made the varsity team and averaged an exceptional twenty points per game over his final two seasons. Now, I'm not downplaying the incredible God-given talent Jordan possesses, but the moral of the story is that if you want to accomplish anything significant, you're going to have to step up and be a real Doer. Michael has said, "I have missed more than nine thousand shots in my career. I have lost almost three hundred games. On twenty-six occasions, I have been entrusted to take the game-winning shot, and I missed. I have failed over and over and over again in my life. And that is why I succeed."

Once you understand what it takes to be a Doer, the question is, in what field do you want to be a Doer? You are the person who takes action and the one who will make a difference in that field. You must concentrate. More than anything else, the field in which you choose to play as a Doer will determine who you are and what you become during your entire lifetime. There are people who set out to be Doers in everything and ultimately accomplish nothing. They soon find that they are unable to truly focus on being exceptional at anything because they have overcommitted themselves. All exceptionally successful people who are Doers in their chosen field are focused intensely.

With this thought in mind, try your hand at developing your own *distinctive competence*. This means to become an expert at something that will make you stand out.

Your Superpowers

Most of us grew up knowing about Superman, Batman, Wonder Woman, and other superheroes. We focused on their physical superpowers, but, in truth, their mental powers are more important. All of these fictional characters have these mental traits in common: They are each on a mission of destiny. They have a burning desire to make a difference and do good. They have a purpose, and action is their duty. They each possess remarkable powers they use to accomplish their goals. They never give up—ever. Can you imagine Superman quitting? Superheroes don't know the meaning of an eight-hour day or a forty-hour workweek. They are passionate for their purpose.

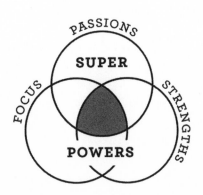

Successful people believe in what they do so passionately that they think about success constantly. For these people, the desire and passion for success has overwhelmed their fear of failure. In other words, they have developed their own superpowers.

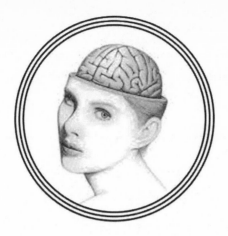

The Power of the Brain

"Sitting on your shoulders is the most complicated object in the known universe."
—Michio Kaku, a futurist and theoretical physicist

Today we are learning incredible new information about the amazing human operating system—the brain. It is a wonder unto itself. According to The National Institute of Health,

The brain is the most complex part of the human body. This three-pound organ is the seat of intelligence, interpreter of the senses, initiator of body movement, and controller of behavior . . . the brain is the source of all the qualities that define our humanity. The brain is the crown jewel of the human body. . . . Scientists have learned more about the brain in the last ten years than in all previous centuries because of the accelerating pace of research in neurological and behavioral science and the development of new research techniques. As a result, Congress named the 1990s the Decade of the Brain.[7]

Here are the specifications of an average human brain:

- It represents about 2 percent of body mass but consumes 20 percent of the body's energy.

- There are a staggering 100,000 miles (528 million feet) of blood vessels in the brain.

- It generates ten to twenty-three watts of electricity—enough to power a light bulb.

- The number of neurons in the brain is estimated at 100 billion, interconnected by an unbelievable 100 trillion synapses.

- The brain's storage capacity is about 2.5 petabytes. A petabyte is 10^{15} bytes of data, 1,000 terabytes, or 1,000,000 gigabytes.

- Generally, people average an amazing 50,000 to 70,000 unique thoughts per day. If you're awake sixteen hours per day, that's 4,375 thoughts per hour.

- When we are asleep, the brain actually consumes more energy than when we are awake. This is because the brain processes the data collected all day when the body is at rest.

- The brain is always learning and adapting.

The brain consists of four core thinking and reasoning areas:

- The left brain is analytical and process oriented.

- The right brain is more creative and intuition-based.

- The emotional, or limbic, system is where we create impulsive thoughts.

- The prefrontal cortex is the decision maker. It processes the inputs from the other three regions of the brain and attempts to come up with well-reasoned, balanced decisions.

Within the brain lives the mind, which is even more fascinating and mysterious. The mind is the consumer of all of the information provided to the brain through all of the brain's receptors. It has the cognitive faculties that enable consciousness, perception, thinking, judgment, and memory, and is the fertile ground where habits, opinions, ideas, and concepts are continually planted.

The mind is where reason is formed and decisions are made. The mind has the ability to talk to itself. The mind lives in more than one dimension. It is the thinking part that makes us who we are through our dreams and desires. We live our lives in our minds. Our bodies and brains make up the factory where the mind lives, thinks, creates, and consumes knowledge. It is where intelligence, personality, and emotions are processed. Nothing has ever been created by humans which did not begin with a thought . . . an idea.

One school of thought is that ideas reside in space and time. They are perhaps unseen molecules that move through space and visit people where they are either grasped and absorbed in the mind or not. If not acted on they may move on through space to visit other minds until finally someone acts on the idea by nurturing it. How many times have you had an idea, mulled it over, and then either dismissed it or forgotten it for some other thought? In her wonderful book, *Big Magic*, Elizabeth Gilbert writes, "I believe that our planet is inhabited not only by animals and plants and bacteria and viruses, but also by *ideas*. Ideas are a disembodied, energetic life form . . . they are completely separate from us but capable of interacting with us—albeit strangely."[8]

We have no idea what invisible forces act all around us, without our knowledge. We know a bit about the most recognizable forces such as gravity, sound waves, light waves, electronic waves, and the atomic and subatomic particles that penetrate seemingly solid materials, but what are the forces we still do not comprehend? Maybe Elizabeth Gilbert is onto something.

We know that each brain is unique in its makeup and abilities. The usual form for measuring cognitive ability is the Intelligence Quotient (IQ) study. The classical IQ test measures several factors of intelligence: logical reasoning, math skills, language abilities, spatial-relations skills, knowledge retained, and the ability to solve novel problems.

Your IQ plays only a small part in your success. Dan Hurley, author of *Smarter: The New Science of Building Brain Power*, believes, "Life is too complicated for any one factor to be the be-all-and-end-all."[9] Fortunately, scientific inquiry has revealed over the years that your intelligence quotient is not a fixed, static characteristic. In fact, it has been proven time and time again that you can improve your intelligence by exercising your brain as you would any other muscle!

When I was released from juvenile hall to join the Air Force, I was tested for intelligence and aptitude. Up to that point, I thought I was not particularly smart. I had grown up with that idea and, having been a total failure so far, it was easy to believe. I was astonished when the evaluator shared my test scores with me. Though I was a high school dropout, my scores indicated that my intellect was at a level commensurate with someone with some college education.

The idea that I was smart was a revelation to me. It took me awhile to finally comprehend this news. This moment of self-awareness changed my life. The only possible reason for such high scores was my insatiable curiosity and a passion for reading. I had learned to escape the pain of an unhappy childhood by keeping my nose in a book as often as possible.

You may be in a similar position, having been made to believe—or worse, explicitly told—you are unintelligent and destined for failure. Do not believe this coming from anybody else. Only your opinion of yourself and your abilities counts. After all, you never know what you're really capable of until you challenge yourself and really try.

According to Edward de Bono, a leading authority in the field of creative thinking and the teaching of thinking as a skill, "Many highly intelligent people are poor thinkers. Many people of average intelligence are skilled thinkers. The [horsepower] of a car is separate from the way the car is driven."

This tells me that raw intelligence alone is not the same as the ability to think clearly, develop plans, and be incredibly persistent. My experience indicates that people of average or slightly above IQ and a high degree of commitment seem to be the most successful at achieving their own measure of success.[10]

Your intellect is like any other muscle, in that you have to exercise it to improve it. The more you use it, the smarter you'll get. There are a few practical ways you can improve your intelligence and thinking skills through hard work: the first and most useful is by reading things that challenge you. Observing through sources other than your personal experience is very important.

In fact, a recent study from the University of California, Berkeley found that students who studied at least one hundred hours for the challenging Law School Admissions Test (LSAT), a comprehensive exam that tests language abilities and logical processing, saw substantial positive changes in the parts of their brains that were responsible for reasoning and thinking.[11]

In my second year of college, I decided that I might want to train as a lawyer, so I took the LSAT and passed it. Just the experience of preparing for and taking the exam was an education. I later decided that even though my grandfather was a lawyer, a career in law was not for me.

Emotional Intelligence

Do you control your emotions or do your emotions control you?

There is now a way to measure your Emotional Intelligence (EI). The study of emotional intelligence came into the mainstream of mental evaluation in the 1990s. It helped explain why people with average IQs can outperform those with higher IQs.

Research now points to emotional intelligence as a critical factor necessary for exceptional success. Emotional intelligence affects how we manage behavior, navigate social complexities, and make personal decisions that achieve positive results. It consists of a flexible set of skills that can be improved with practice. Although some people are naturally more emotionally intelligent than others, you can develop high emotional intelligence even if you aren't born with it.

According to writer and educator Kendra Cherry, this refers to the ability to perceive, control, and evaluate emotions. Research suggests that emotional intelligence can be learned and strengthened. So can your ability to understand, interpret, and respond to the emotions of others. Your Emotional Quotient measures your ability to manage your own behavior and control your emotions at times when other people might become irrational, impulsive, or compulsive. That is the very definition of emotional maturity.[12]

It is incredibly important to cultivate the ability to understand how you are interacting with another person, and have the humble, self-disciplined ability to realize that, on some occasions, you need to change your behavior. You usually can't change the behavior of others, but you must be willing to exercise the self-discipline to make the change in your own mind and rein in your emotions.

A large part of utilizing your EI is knowing which emotions are appropriate to the current circumstance. For example, I've used both anger and compassion as management tools when I felt that those emotions might be helpful.

The best seller *Emotional Intelligence: Why It Can Matter More Than IQ*, by Dr. Daniel Goleman, a Harvard-educated psychologist and two-time Pulitzer Prize nominee, offers startling insights into our "two minds"—the rational and the emotional—and how they together shape our destiny.

Goleman asserts that perhaps the most important thing we can develop in ourselves and in our children is emotional intelligence, arguing that our ability to learn is directly related to our emotional intelligence.[13]

Like most people, I can lose control of my emotions when I feel threatened or frustrated. That is the precise time when emotional control would serve me best.

Most of us have had experiences with people who get caught up in the heat of the moment and lose control. Whether it stems from work or family stress, a political or religious debate, or even sports, usually this results in someone saying things they should never have said, all because they allowed impulse to take over, as opposed to keeping a cool head. In many cases, this behavior is accompanied by consumption of mind-altering drugs or alcohol.

I don't know about you, but it's difficult for me to relate to someone who flies off the handle. It becomes one-sided, and that kind of impulsive behavior is usually a relationship killer. Most of us react far better to people with the skills of compassion and empathy. One of the marks of people with fantastic EI is that they make you feel as though you are the only person in the room when you're speaking with them.

One example that showed me President Clinton's power of EI was a conversation I had with former Republican Speaker of the House Newt Gingrich at a reception for a retiring congressman. Gingrich confessed to me that he "loved Bill Clinton." When I asked him why he was constantly attacking President Clinton, he responded by reminding me that it was his job, but he still liked him immensely. Imagine that. Despite being quite ideologically different, on the opposite side of most issues, and rarely missing an opportunity to tear each other down (publicly, at least), President Clinton was able to transcend a host of glaring relational challenges and convince Speaker Gingrich that he wasn't so bad after all. That's some impressive emotional intelligence, in my opinion.

What's the secret to this kind of emotional success? First, try to understand what's motivating the person with whom you're interacting instead of what's motivating you. Why? You already know what you want. What you don't know is what the other party wants. After spending years negotiating as part of my business endeavors, I have found that the real challenge lies in coming to the table with a mindset geared toward figuring out what the other side wants and trying to find a way to help them walk away with what they want, while at the same time walking away with what you want.

When negotiating a very large land purchase several years ago, I first tried the friendly neighbor approach and would regularly visit the owner of several hundred acres on his porch over several months. I later found that other suitors were doing the same. I then told him that if he was ready to sell he should ask for best offers from each potential buyer and then call me. I promised that I would be more creative and I would make him an offer that would prove to be his best choice by far. If I could not improve his deal with the best offer, then I would help him negotiate the best terms with whomever he chose. He agreed because he trusted me and I ended up giving him substantially more than he had hoped for in the beginning.

Going into a negotiation, or any kind of a relationship, with an adversarial position ("What can I get from this?") turns out to be a poor way of negotiating and a poor way to relate to your significant other, friends, neighbors, and coworkers.

Ultimately, the importance of Emotional Intelligence is best summed up by our friend Daniel Goleman, who also wrote in a piece in the *Harvard Business Review* that the most effective leaders are alike in one crucial way:

They all have a high degree of what has come to be known as *emotional intelligence*. It's not that IQ and technical skills are irrelevant. They do matter, but mainly as "threshold capabilities;" that is, they are the entry-level requirements for executive positions. But my research, along with other recent studies, clearly shows that emotional intelligence is the sine qua non of leadership. Without it, a person can have the best training in the world, an incisive, analytical mind, and an endless supply of smart ideas, but he still won't make a great leader.[14]

Getting to know your Emotional Intelligence (EI) and understanding how to harness your various emotions will help you achieve your life goals as much or more than any other single thing.

Personality Profiles

Most people cannot accurately describe their own personality. If you've never taken a personality inventory, I highly recommend you do so. It's important to understand how you think and react to others. I am by nature an outgoing person and have benefited from using this trait to my advantage over my lifetime.

A personality is much like a rubber band. You can bend or stretch it to become different for a while, but with time it will go back to its normal style. I have learned that once a person reaches his or her mid-twenties, personality is generally set. The sooner you learn to work with your strongest personality traits and avoid your weakest traits, the better equipped you will be to succeed.

Recently, a friend came to me for advice about what he should do next. He is fifty years old and was depressed because he could no longer do the physical work he had relied on for his whole career. I helped him inventory his personality characteristics. We both decided his strongest positive traits were his gift of gab, his ability to "never meet a stranger," and his knowledge and experience in the craftsmen trades, including carpentry, plumbing, electrical, and design. He developed a new outlook on his future and decided he wanted to be employed in a home improvement center, where he could spend productive days helping people with their projects.

In my mid-thirties, I was given the Myers-Briggs Type Indicator test as part of the hiring process and found it to be a wonderful tool in the quest to better understand my own personality's strengths and weaknesses. Isabel Briggs Myers said, "Whatever the circumstances of your life, the understanding of (personality) type can make your perceptions clearer, your judgments sounder, and your life closer to your heart's desire." In my case, knowing my characteristics and preferences has helped me negotiate better and work more closely with my employees to keep them motivated.

The purpose of the test is to make the personality types pioneered by psychiatrist and psychotherapist Carl Jung more accessible and useful to the general population, based on the theory that most random human behavior is actually based on an orderly set of preferences related to basic differences in how people prefer to utilize their perception and judgment. The Myers and Briggs Foundation explains it this way:

> Perception involves all the ways of becoming aware of things, people, happenings, or ideas. Judgment involves all the ways of coming to conclusions about what has been perceived. If people differ systematically in what they perceive and in how they reach conclusions, then it

is only reasonable for them to differ correspondingly in their interests, reactions, values, motivations, and skills.[15]

The Myers-Briggs test reveals sixteen different personality types, broken down into combinations of the four areas defined by the following letters:

- **How you interact with the world**: E or I, Extraversion (others) or Introversion (self)

- **Information you notice and remember**: S or N, Sensing (facts/details) or Intuition (imagination)

- **How you make decisions**: T or F, Thinking (objective) or Feeling (subjective)

- **How you prefer to live**: J or P, Judging (order/structure) or Perceiving (spontaneous)

There are sixteen personality types identified based on different combinations of the above temperament traits, and there is success potential in every one of the personality types. No certain profile is any better or worse than another. The trick is to understand your own personality and bend your behavior to favor your personal strengths. Knowing your own temperament and fitting your pursuits to it are essential to becoming extraordinary. For some, it will come naturally, but for many others it will require an extra focus.

I've outlined the sixteen patterns. Try to fit yourself into the pattern that you believe most describes you in your own opinion. Make note of your choice and then go online and take the Myers-Briggs test ($50). Also, visualize which of these patterns might fit people you know well. As you read each pattern, try to think of someone you know who epitomizes the description. Write their name next to the pattern. When you better understand those around you, then you have a better chance of influencing them.

The Sixteen Patterns

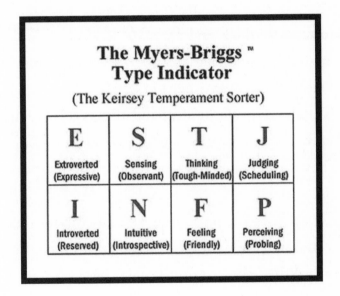

INTP

(Introverted Thinking with Intuition)

These people are the Thinkers and are fairly rare. They take pride in their inventiveness and creativity and have a vigorous mind. Usually known as the philosopher, the architect, or the absent-minded professor, INTPs have been responsible for many scientific discoveries.

Examples: physicist Albert Einstein, Microsoft cofounder Paul Allen, and Wikipedia founder Jimmy Wales

ENTP
(Extroverted Intuition with Thinking)

These people are the Visionaries, and their primary interest in life is to understand the world that they live in. They absorb ideas and images about the situations they observe. Using their intuition strength to process this information, they are usually quick and accurate in their ability to size up a situation. They have a deeper understanding of their environment than most other personality types.

Since they generally understand things quickly and with great depth, they are usually flexible and adapt well to varying tasks. They are generally good at almost anything that interests them.

These are idea people who get excited about their ideas and are able to spread their enthusiasm to others to get the support that they need to fulfill their visions.

Examples: President Barack Obama, Apple cofounder Steve Wozniak, actor Neil Patrick Harris, and talk-show host Bill Maher

ENTJ
(Extroverted Thinking with Intuition)

These people are the Executives and are natural leaders who often take charge. They usually have a clear vision for the future and intuitively understand how to move people and processes toward that goal. They tend to approach every situation with the attitude of an efficiency analyst and are not shy about pointing out what could be done better.

ENTJs are gregarious and quickly have ideas for how a person will fit into their grand scheme. They are typically direct and may seem presumptuous or even arrogant. These people can size people and situations up very quickly but also have trouble being less than honest about what they see. ENTJs seek people in powerful influence positions. They are ambitious and often can be described as workaholics. More than any other personality type, they enjoy their work. The ENTJ type on average earns the most money.[16]

Examples: Apple cofounder Steve Jobs and former governor of Florida Jeb Bush

INTJ
(Introverted Intuition with Thinking)

This is the rarest of personality types. These people are the Scientists and are reserved and serious critical thinkers. They are curious about the world around them and want to know the principle behind everything. When asked a question, they will consider it and present a complex answer. They can be blunt in their presentation.

These people are not usually gregarious by nature and tend to have a self-assured manner based on their strong opinion of their own intelligence. They speak with confidence and expect others to see the wisdom in their perceptions. They enjoy discussing ideas but may get themselves into trouble because if someone's beliefs don't make logical sense, they have no qualms about pointing that out.

Examples: chess champion Bobby Fischer, President Dwight Eisenhower, former Federal Reserve Chairman Alan Greenspan, physicist Stephen Hawking, Facebook CEO Mark Zuckerberg, and PayPal cofounder Elon Musk

ENFP
(Extroverted Intuition with Feeling)

This person is the Inspirer and is a free spirit and can be the life of the party. Inspirers enjoy the social and emotional connections they make with others and can talk their way into or out of anything. They love life, seeing it as a special gift, and strive to make the most of it. Most individuals within this personality type have great people skills.

Examples: actor Robin Williams, Walt Disney, and WikiLeaks founder Julian Assange

INFP
(Introverted Feeling with Intuition)

These people are the Idealists and are cool on the outside. They reserve their real thoughts and feelings only for people they know well. They are often spiritual and interested in having meaningful conversations about values, ethics, people, and personal growth. They are passionate about their ideals, but private as well. These types make talented writers, but may be uncomfortable expressing themselves verbally. Being generally thoughtful and considerate makes them good listeners. INFPs do not like conflict.

Example: playwright William Shakespeare, author J. K. Rowling, and artist Vincent van Gogh

ENFJ
(Extroverted Feeling with Intuition)

These types are the Givers, and people generally love them because they are so people-focused and charming. They hate to be alone and may feel lonely even when surrounded by people. They get great satisfaction from serving others. Their people skills are extraordinary. They are fun to be with, and truly love people. They are typically straightforward and honest, and exude a lot of self-confidence. They are generally bright, full of potential, energetic, and fast paced.

Examples: Reverend Martin Luther King Jr., President Abraham Lincoln, President Ronald Reagan, and television star and executive Oprah Winfrey

INFJ
(Introverted Intuition with Feeling)

These people are the Protectors and are gentle, caring, complex, and intuitive. They live in a world of hidden meanings and possibilities. They are typically artistic and creative. Though soft-spoken, they have very strong opinions and will fight tirelessly for an idea they believe in. They are decisive and strong willed but will rarely use that energy for personal gain. Some will think of this type person as a quiet extrovert. This person needs time alone to decompress and recharge.

Examples: President Thomas Jefferson, Holocaust survivor Elie Wiesel, leader of Nationalist China Chiang Kai-shek, psychiatrist Carl Gustav Jung, actor Daniel Day-Lewis, and musician George Harrison of the Beatles

ESTJ
(Extroverted Thinking with Sensation)

These people are the Guardians and are usually model citizens and pillars of the community. They take their commitments seriously and follow their own standards of "good citizenship" to the letter. These people enjoy interacting with others and like to have fun. They must be careful not to be too rigid or overly detail oriented. Since they put a lot of weight in their own beliefs, it's important that they remember to value other people's input and opinions. If they neglect their feeling side, they may have a problem fulfilling others' needs for intimacy and may unknowingly hurt people's feelings by applying logic and reason to situations that demand more subjective reasoning.

Examples: former Secretary of State Hillary Clinton, psychologist and talk-show host Dr. Phil, First Lady Michelle Obama, businesswoman Martha Stewart, and Christian evangelist Billy Graham

ISTJ
(Introverted Sensation with Thinking)

These people are the Duty-Fulfillers and are thought to be the most numerous. Their defining characteristics are integrity, practical logic, and dedication to duty. They tend to uphold traditions and rules. These people take responsibility for their actions, and take pride in their work.

Examples: President Richard Nixon, Queen Elizabeth II, Amazon founder Jeff Bezos, and investor Warren Buffett

ESFJ
(Extroverted Feeling with Sensation)

These types are the Caregivers and are people persons. They want to be liked and are truly interested in others, gathering detailed information about them in order to be supportive. They can bring out the best in people and are empathetic and good at reading others. In general, people like to be around ESFJs.

These types are very dependable and value security and stability.

Examples: Pope Francis, Prince William, former Governor of Alaska Sarah Palin, and singer-songwriter Elton John

ISFJ
(Introverted Sensation with Feeling)

These people are the Nurturers and are characterized by their desire to serve others. They need to be needed. In some cases, this need is so strong that the usual give-and-take relationships can be unsatisfying to them. Sometimes, these people may be taken for granted or even be taken advantage of by others.

Examples: President Jimmy Carter, President George H. W. Bush, Mother Teresa, and Prince Charles

ESTP

(Extroverted Sensation with Thinking)

These types are the Doers and their focus is on action in the moment. They solve practical problems quickly. These people are excellent in emergencies, when they can apply their quick logic to situations where action is necessary. Long-term goals are far less interesting to them.

According to psychiatrist David Keirsey, "None are as socially sophisticated as they, none as suave and polished—and none such master manipulators of the people around them."[17]

Since they are typically well coordinated, many are natural athletes. They like to use this physical aptitude in the pursuit of excitement and adventure and enjoy putting their skills to the test in risky or even dangerous activities.

Examples: President Theodore Roosevelt, President Franklin D. Roosevelt, real estate mogul Donald Trump, self-help author Stephen R. Covey, and musician Taylor Swift

ISTP
(Introverted Thinking with Sensation)

These people are the Mechanics and are highly logical. They enjoy learning by experience. Self-confident and easy-going, they are action-oriented. They love excitement and new experiences. People with this personality type can be difficult to get to know, often because they are focused so much on action and results, rather than on emotions.

Examples: astronaut Alan Shepard, aviator Amelia Earhart, and golfer Tiger Woods

ESFP
(Extroverted Sensation with Feeling)

These people are the Performers and live in the world of people possibilities. They love new experiences. They are lively and fun, and enjoy being the center of attention. They live in the here-and-now and relish excitement and drama in their lives. They have very strong interpersonal skills and can enjoy the role of peacemaker. Since they make decisions by using their personal values, they are usually very sympathetic and concerned for other people's well-being.

Examples: President John F. Kennedy, magazine publisher Hugh Hefner, Starbucks CEO Howard Schultz, and self-help author Tony Robbins

ISFP

(Introverted Feeling with Sensation)

These people are the Artists. They live in a colorful, sensual world, inspired by connections with people and ideas. They are in tune with the way things look, taste, sound, feel, and smell. They are likely to be animal lovers and do not like the limelight. These people can seem unpredictable, even to their close friends and loved ones. These types cannot take criticism well and will end relationships over even a small perceived slight.

Examples: former First Lady Jacqueline Kennedy Onassis, Princess Diana, musician Paul McCartney of the Beatles, and performers Michael Jackson, Barbra Streisand, and Lady Gaga

———

Those who know me will not be surprised to learn I am an ENTJ, a.k.a. the Confident General—the Business Executive—the Ambitious Workaholic.

Steve Jobs, another ENTJ, famously said in his 2005 commencement speech at Stanford University, "Your time is limited, so don't waste it living someone else's life. Don't be trapped by dogma—which is living with the results of other people's thinking. Don't let the noise of others' opinions drown out your own inner voice. And most important, have the courage to follow your heart and intuition. They somehow already know what you truly want to become. Everything else is secondary."

Over the years, I have used this personality assessment tool for all potential new employees. It is a broad view of a person's overall personality biases. When choosing people to help you achieve your goals, it is always better to find those with personality traits best suited to the position you are trying to fill.

When one of my accountants came to me some years back and said, "I want to be a leasing agent. They make more money than I do, and their job seems like it would be something I can easily do." I explained how being in a job that aligned most closely to her strongest traits gave her the best chance at success. Her personality type, ISTJ, was much better aligned with her current position. She was disappointed and envious of the others in leasing. Within months, she was gone, and I had lost a good accountant.

The next time this happened, one of my property managers asked if he could become a project manager. Once again, he was interested in earning more money. I went through the same story about his personality alignment ISFJ (nurturers who are characterized by their desire to serve others) with the job, but this time when he kept pushing, I said, "Let's do this. I will pay to send you to a Dale Carnegie course on *How to Win Friends & Influence People*." He started the course and lost interest partway through. He was a good property manager and stayed with me for years.

The Myers-Briggs personality assessment hasn't just been helpful for my company and employees; it's been a tremendous help for me personally. I didn't know that I was an ENTJ until my business partner, John, had me tested prior to the formation of our partnership. I was thirty-eight years old when I took the test, and I had never heard of it. It described exactly who I am, but more important, it also served as a validation of what had made me successful to that point.

The Myers-Briggs test taught me which aspects of my personality had gotten me to where I was and helped me identify which traits to magnify and foster. It was a powerful force in learning to build on my strengths, including some I didn't even know I had before that point.

I would strongly encourage you to pursue greater self-knowledge by figuring out the strengths and weaknesses of your personality. If you want to succeed in fulfilling your Grand Vision, it will be useful for you to know which traits will get you across the finish line and onto your next Grand Vision. You might be surprised at what you find. You can either go online and take the assessment yourself, or find a good consultant who can help you. Either way, stop waiting, and start exploring what makes you *you*!

Mental Flexibility and Enthusiasm

Some would say, as we grow in maturity we should leave behind some of the idealism and youthful passions of our younger days. This is how most people think of aging. However, it turns out that in a rapidly changing environment, retaining our youthful flexibility and enthusiasm can provide the tools we need to succeed. According to Bruce Charlton, a doctor and psychology professor at Newcastle University, youthful behavior in adulthood is actually a valuable developmental characteristic, which he calls psychological neoteny. According to Dr. Charlton, human beings now take longer to reach mental maturity and, he says, "A flexibility of attitudes, behaviors, and knowledge may be as useful in navigating the instability of the modern world, where people are more likely to change jobs, learn new skills, and move to new places."

Having a young mind can be defined by two categories: "mental qualities" and "mental attitudes." Your "mental qualities" are things like sharpness, memory, and problem-solving ability, all key traits for succeeding personally and professionally. I'll go into more detail on this topic later on, but many people believe that your mental qualities are somehow fixed, a belief that I have come to realize is patently false. In fact, whatever your estimation of your mental abilities, improvement can almost always be made through effort.[18]

Your "mental attitudes" are even more important. Thomas Jefferson, one of the United States' greatest founding fathers and presidents, once said, "Nothing can stop the man with the right mental attitude from achieving his goal;

nothing on earth can help the man with the wrong mental attitude."

This truism applies not only to your professional life but to every other aspect of your life. I believe that the most reliable predictor of success is the willingness to remain positive in the face of challenging circumstances, and that maintaining that positivity is the most valuable trait of a young mind. There is nothing you can't face with the right outlook and the willingness to embrace change.

Your Learning Style

Have you ever struggled to learn something fairly simple and failed? When others around you are getting the lessons and moving on, you might feel left behind and can begin to think you might not be as smart.

But here's the good news. Recent research has shown that the human brain receives information and processes it using several different learning methods and styles.[19] The brain also changes the way you internalize experiences, the way you recall information, and even the words you choose. Each learning style uses different parts of the brain. Researchers using brain-imaging technologies have been able to discover the key areas of the brain responsible for each learning style. Here are some of the currently recognized styles of learning:

- **Visual:** to learn by seeing information, pictures, and images. These people think in 3-D and have great imaginations. Sailors, sculptors, painters, engineers, pilots, designers, architects, and surgeons are usually visual learners. Think Leonardo da Vinci, Pablo Picasso, and Frank Lloyd Wright.

- **Auditory:** to receive knowledge through sound. If you are an auditory learner, you will use sound, rhyme, and music in your learning. Auditory learners remember what they hear and say, and enjoy classroom and small-group discussion. They understand information best when they hear it. Think Elvis Presley and Tony DeBlois.

- **Verbal:** to receive knowledge through words, both in speech and writing. These people usually gravitate toward the following occupations: writer, speaker, actor, teacher, lawyer, and politician. Think Jerry Seinfeld, T. S. Eliot, and Ernest Hemingway.

- **Tactile:** to learn through touching and doing, activity/motion, hands-on, experimental, and participative. Occupations include athlete, dancer, actor, performer, and coach. Think Kobe Bryant and Babe Ruth.

- **Logical:** to respond to logic, reasoning, and systems. These people prefer reason, analysis, logic, and numbers. They are problem solvers, and can identify patterns. Occupations include mathematician, scientist, accountant, banker, inventor, detective, and engineer. Think Neil deGrasse Tyson, Charles Darwin, and Carl Sagan.

- **Social:** to prefer to learn in an environment that includes interaction with other people. Teacher, salesperson, social worker, counselor, doctor, nurse, and psychiatrist. Think the Dalai Lama, Barbara Walters, and Jimmy Carter.

- **Solitary or Self-taught:** to prefer to work alone and use self-study. They are also known as autodidacts. Occupations include researcher, author, philosopher, and explorer. Think Socrates, Sigmund Freud, and Plato.

We all use combinations of learning styles, but one style will be your dominant and best style. I have found that my preferred styles of learning are solitary, visual, and logical.

Traditional educational institutions primarily use verbal and logical teaching methods and still rely on presentation, repetition, rote memorization, and examinations for reinforcement. As a result, we label those who respond well to verbal and logical learning styles and are proficient at memorization as smart. Conversely, students who are better at other learning styles often find themselves not performing as well, even though they are as smart as or smarter than the higher performers.

As a youth, Albert Einstein clashed with authorities and resented his school's regimen and teaching methods. He later wrote that "the spirit of learning and creative thought were lost in strict rote learning."

When Einstein sat for the entrance examinations for college, he failed in the general part of the examination but obtained exceptional grades in physics and mathematics, areas where he was acting as a solitary and logical learner. He would later say, "Most teachers waste their time by asking questions that are intended to discover what a pupil does not know, whereas the true art of questioning is to discover what the pupil does know or is capable of knowing."

By recognizing and understanding your own natural learning preferences, you can use the learning techniques best suited to you. This improves the speed and quality of your learning.

It seems that each brain contains what can be considered gifts and challenges. A good friend of mine, Tony DeBlois,[20] was born blind and weighed just one pound and three-quarters of an ounce. It was later determined he is also autistic. But Tony, now forty-one years old, is also an autistic prodigious savant, one of fewer than one hundred of these people known in the world. He has been playing the piano since age two, and thanks to his dedicated mother and teacher, Janice, today he plays more than twenty musical instruments, including strings, percussion, and wind. Tony has an amazing musical repertoire of more than ten thousand songs covering every genre. He can sing in eight languages. In addition, he is perhaps the nicest person I've ever met.

Tony is a perfect example of someone understanding his unique strengths and using them to overcome what others see as weaknesses. He knows himself and uses that Power for good. You may not have the same strengths Tony has, but it's also unlikely you face challenges as dramatic. What you do have in common is an ability to understand your strengths and weaknesses, and adapt to them to give yourself the best chance for success.

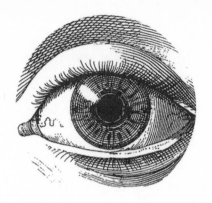

The Power of Vision

"As a child, I watched Dallas and that was my vision for my life for as long as I could remember."
—Will Smith, actor, producer, and Grammy winner

Knowing yourself prepares you to work toward success, but actually achieving success requires direction—a goal to work toward and a plan for getting there. That's where the Power of Vision comes into play.

Many consider daydreaming a waste of time, but I disagree. We would be far worse off if artist Jean-Michel Basquiat or ballet dancer Wendy Whelan had never daydreamed. Bill Clinton once said to me, "To succeed, spend your best time thinking about tomorrows, not yesterdays."

It is estimated that we spend one-third of our waking hours daydreaming.[21] During that time, the mind is very active. Marcus Raichle, a neurologist and radiologist at Washington University, sums it up: "When your brain is supposedly doing nothing and daydreaming, it's really doing a tremendous amount. We call it 'resting state,' but the brain isn't resting at all."[22] Daydreaming is fine as long as you then follow up with action.

Your Thinking Place

Go to your most solitary place to allow your mind to wander. For some, it might be a long walk or a private drive. Others prefer a favorite chair or room. I prefer sitting at the base of a tree in the woods without any distractions other than nature at its finest. I like to just sit and watch nature unfold and encircle me.

Think of a date in the far future. It may be ten or twenty years, or more. I prefer to think in decades, because it allows me time to accomplish big things. Now, visualize who and what you are by then and why. Another way of seeking a vision of your future is to think about your funeral. What do you hope your friends and family will remember you for?

This is your Grand Vision, a call to action that defines in clear terms what your vision for success means to you.

Now, write your Grand Vision down and carry it with you. A written vision statement is far more powerful than one that is not written. In the next chapter, you will read about why written statements are more effective than mental commitments.

My first Grand Vision came to me while I was on guard duty late one evening while in the Air Force and it was that I must rebuild my family's lost fortune. I decided my Grand Vision would be to

"Rebuild my family's wealth and reputation."

Perhaps you want to be one who changes the world. Perhaps you are driven to be a great concert pianist. You might want to be an incredible evangelist. Or you might aspire to become financially independent or governor of your state. Just think—while you're still in high school, you could decide you want to become president of the United States. That's exactly what Bill Clinton did in his teen years as a poor kid from Arkansas. He went on to become the forty-second president.

My next Grand Vision was in 1989, when I was on safari in Botswana and crept to a watering hole before sunup one crisp morning, armed only with a camera and a bottle of water. I hid behind some brush and watched first the antelope and warthogs approach the water hole with great trepidation. There was barely enough light to see more than ten feet but I was thrilled to be a part of their world. Later, the larger animals came in, and the smaller ones left. Finally, the lions came, and the rest scattered, but not too far.

At the time, I had a successful business in partnership with John, who was seventeen years my senior, who I admired greatly. I had achieved both my twenty-year and thirty-year goals and was financially independent, so I decided rather than chase more wealth for wealth's sake, I needed a new Grand Vision. I needed a course change because there seemed to be something missing in my life. While in Africa, I decided my next Grand Vision would be to

"Develop and maintain balance in my life."

My definition of balance was to spend one-third of my time working, one-third on faith and family, and one-third playing. I started rearranging my life to achieve this balance. It took six months of color-coding my appointment calendar by the three categories to finally adjust my priorities, and it was worth it.

In 1999, I developed the third Grand Vision as my wife, Joan, and I were flying to Africa so I could take up my new post as US ambassador to a regional embassy, serving Mauritius, the Seychelles, and the Comoros, all Indian Ocean island nations off the southeast coast of Africa. Sitting there in the darkness and solitude, as my wife slept next to me, it all came together in my mind. I turned to wake Joan and told her I knew our mission for this chapter of our lives:

"Make a difference, do good, and have fun."

I told her, "if we measure everything we attempt to accomplish by these standards, we will feel a real sense of accomplishment."

She said, "Great," and rolled over to go back to sleep.

Joan and I were able to fulfill this Grand Vision in the coming years in ways we couldn't have imagined at the time.

You will remember that the first tenet of my Grand Vision was "make a difference." Looking back on my experiences as the US ambassador to Mauritius, the Seychelles, and the Comoros, one of my greatest successes in making a difference came as a result of a groundbreaking trade fair in Mauritius.

As part of promoting regional stability, democracy, and free markets on the continent of Africa, as well as building the friendship between Mauritius and the United States, it was determined that the central focus (Grand Vision) of my time there would be economic development. I created an ambitious and unprecedented economic development plan with a focus on attracting American businesses to the country.

We set a goal of drawing the attention of American businesses to Mauritius and its democratic, free-enterprise culture as a business gateway to all of sub-Saharan Africa, much like Dubai is to the Middle East.

To accomplish this goal, we decided to put on a large regional trade fair to highlight the country's many benefits with the cooperation of the Mauritius government. We then promoted this plan all over the world to garner interest and support. The event lasted a week, and was a tremendous success. In fact, two hundred American companies were represented, and sixty thousand visitors from fifteen countries were in attendance.

Additionally, six hundred tons of American goods were sold during the fair, and it turned out to be the largest trade fair ever conducted by the State Department anywhere in Africa. The end result of our efforts far surpassed anything we imagined. We successfully secured an average of one regional office operation for a major US corporation per month, including companies such as IBM, Hewlett-Packard, Dell, CitiTrust, and Gateway.

The long-term positive impact of this growth is still an encouraging reminder of what can happen by staying committed to a Grand Vision.

The second tenet of my Grand Vision is to "do good." Doing good and making a difference go hand-in-hand, meaning that acting for the benefit of others always has a positive impact, even if it is only on oneself. You can make a difference in a negative sense, of course, but doing good should never result in a negative impact. That was certainly the case for my efforts to "do good" by securing a coveted spot on the UN Security Council for Mauritius, against steep odds.

The Security Council is a critical international body because it has several crucial functions in an increasingly challenging global society, including taking the lead in determining the existence of a threat to the peace or an act of aggression. It calls upon the parties in a dispute to settle it by peaceful means and recommends methods of adjustment or terms of settlement. In some cases, the Security Council can resort to imposing sanctions or even authorize the use of force to maintain or restore international peace and security.

The Security Council also recommends to the General Assembly the appointment of the Secretary-General and the admission of new members to the United Nations. And, together with the General Assembly, it elects the judges of the International Court of Justice.[23]

In 2000, it was time to elect a new member from Africa to the UN Security Council and Sudan was the next in line. But the United States was opposed to its joining the Council because of Sudan's human rights abuses, including the bombing of UN relief sites.

Assistant Secretary of State Susan Rice, who went on to serve as President Obama's national security adviser, approached me to ask if Mauritius would be interested in challenging Sudan for the spot. I approached the Prime Minister Navin Ramgoolam with what I thought was the chance of a lifetime for a small nation like Mauritius, a chance to step up as a leader, not just in Africa, but around the world.

He took a week to think it over, and he returned with the conviction that he would agree to put Mauritius forward (despite opposition from his deputy prime minister and his ambassador to the UN) if he could count on the full support of the United States. I reassured him that the country of Mauritius would, indeed, have our support.

After a coordinated effort between the State Department and Mauritius to rally support locally and internationally, we were ready to take our case to the full UN for a vote. We had successfully disrupted the consensus vote for Sudan and created a tremendous opportunity. Unfortunately, we failed to foresee one problem that almost ruined our hopes and plans.

For some reason, Ramgoolam decided that September 2000, in the middle of this process, was a good time to try for a second term, so he called for a snap election and was soundly defeated. He was perplexed by his defeat, and he asked me, "What went wrong, Mr. Ambassador?" I told him, "You hired French consultants to guide your campaign against the first candidate of French descent in the history of Mauritius. The French consultants gave you terrible advice and perhaps sabotaged your candidacy. Never underestimate French pride."

(It's interesting to note that when Ramgoolam decided to run for the office again in 2005, he called me for advice on whom he should hire as his political consultant for the campaign. He took my advice and was reelected.)

Ramgoolam's defeat meant that we had to go through the process of selling UN Security Council membership all over again, a prospect that could have been far more daunting than it turned out to be. Fortunately for us, the new prime minister, Sir Anerood Jugnauth, asked only for my assurance that the attempt would be successful, and I assured him sincerely that we together would succeed.

This was a precarious situation, both for the United States and for Mauritius. But Mauritius was taking a gamble by challenging Sudan at all. Mauritius's candidacy was extremely unpopular with a few nations in Africa. Had Sir Anerood doubted my sincerity for only a moment he would have pulled the plug on our joint effort.

Fortunately, Mauritius received the necessary two-thirds vote after another coordinated effort between the American mission at the UN, the State Department, and our embassy. It took four rounds of voting, but I was delighted to see Mauritius join the UN Security Council in January 2001. This was definitely a watershed moment for the nation of Mauritius, and I am glad to have had the privilege of helping in the process. I was excited to be able to do good by advancing the cause of a wonderful nation like Mauritius and its people. And for its part, Sudan has not joined the Security Council since its defeat that year.

When it comes to the third and final tenet of my Grand Vision, "have fun," there were ample opportunities to fulfill that during my time as ambassador. One of the best parts of being an ambassador is the chance to mix business and pleasure on a regular basis. A large part of the job description is getting immersed in local culture, experiencing local traditions, socializing with fascinating people, and going to lively and enjoyable dinner parties and receptions.

It's safe to say that Joan and I had a blast serving our country, and were privileged to spend time in such a rewarding and fun position. It can also be fun to help others have fun, something I was able to accomplish by creating an increase in scheduled naval visits to Seychelles from three per year to a minimum of once a month, resulting in an economic boost of at least $1 million per ship visit to the economy of Seychelles, and a welcome respite for US Navy sailors lucky enough to come through the area.

The people of the Seychelles certainly enjoyed the economic growth, and I know that the sailors enjoyed their time in such a beautiful place. It made me happy to know that I was able to provide a little bit of extra happiness to a lot of people with such a simple accomplishment.

As we left our post in Mauritius in March 2001, Joan and I reflected on that Grand Vision I relayed to her on our first plane ride there in 1999, and we felt a strong sense of satisfaction that we had fully embraced and succeeded in following that creed.

Since we left our diplomatic post, I have had numerous opportunities to continue living out my Grand Vision to "make a difference, do good, and have fun" through both personal and business dealings and diplomatic missions around the world.

In February 2012, I was invited to travel to Cuba with twenty-seven other former American ambassadors on a historic trip to begin the effort to improve relations with our neighbor to the south. This had been a years-long effort that was now coming to fruition. The government was beginning to loosen the restrictions on private business ownership. A few small businesses and restaurants were open when we were there. We discovered at that time there was a willingness to embrace change on the part of this secretive government.

Foreign investment in the Cuban tourism sector was increasing steadily, made possible due to constitutional changes to allow for the recognition of foreign-held capital.

After the visit I wrote in my report, "It seems to me that Cuba is moving toward an economic and governance model similar to the command controlled, market-based system operating in China. I am hopeful we in the United States make the necessary changes to bring Cuba closer to us. If we are not willing to loosen our grip on the past, we will be inviting other nations less like us to have a stronghold just ninety miles off our shores. Hopefully our leadership will learn from our mistakes of the past."

In 2014 President Obama took a major step toward ending the fifty-five-year embargo by announcing the "normalization" of the US relationship with Cuba.

In 2015 our Council of American Ambassadors delegation was invited back by the Cuban government. Since our visit in 2012, great progress had been made in every area. More importantly, the people we met were uniformly optimistic about the changes.

Even some of the old guard seems to be coming around to the realization that there might be a better way for their people. The time may be right to finally end the animosity with our closest offshore neighbor. There is a lot at stake for both sides. We must never allow Cuba to again fall under the control of a potential enemy of the US. I predict a bright future for our neighbor to the south.

This goes back to that Grand Vision I established on the way to Mauritius with my wife, and today my Grand Vision remains exactly the same but with a special clause:

"Make a Difference—Do Good—Have Fun—and Never Retire."

Grand Vision Profiles

Many people find it difficult to fully form their Grand Vision, or at least put it into words. I could go on and on about the importance of one's Grand Vision but I have found it's most helpful when you observe it close-up for yourself by reading a biography or documentary on a person where their life is put into focus. Just pick someone, anyone, who inspires you to chase that Grand Vision, get to know them (in person, by word-of-mouth, or even on Wikipedia!), and figure out what you can learn from them that will help you chase your goals and dreams. Here I've profiled a few people I admire, primarily as forerunners to pursuing one's Grand Vision. I consider many of them friends and mentors, despite having never met some of them. Their example of strong and single-minded pursuit of their goals provides worthy examples of the traits I believe are worth cultivating in your life. In short, the following are people who successfully pursued their Grand Vision.

Jack Ma (1964–)
Founder of Alibaba
2014 richest man in China
(*Forbes*, September 9, 2014)

Jack Ma was born in Hangzhou, China. As a youth, he wanted to learn English, so he rode his bike each morning to a nearby hotel to talk with foreigners and would guide them around the city free so he could practice his English.

He wanted to go on to Hangzhou Normal University but failed the entrance exam—twice. Refusing to give up, on the third attempt, he passed and went on to be elected student chairman and graduated in 1988 with a bachelor's degree in English. He later became a lecturer in English and international trade at the Hangzhou Dianzi University.

Ma first started building websites for Chinese companies with the help of friends in the United States. He said, "The day we got connected to the World Wide Web, I invited friends over to my house, and on a very slow dial-up connection, we waited three and a half hours and got half a page . . . We drank, watched TV, and played cards, waiting. But I was so proud. I had proved the Internet existed."

In 1995, Ma founded China Yellowpages, widely believed to be China's first Internet-based company. In 1998, he headed an information technology company established by the Ministry of Foreign Trade and Economic Cooperation. In 1999, he decided to quit his job and founded Alibaba, a China-based business-to-business marketplace, in his apartment with a group of seventeen friends. After ten long years of hard work, by 2009, Ma was honored by *Time* magazine with inclusion into the *Time* list of the world's "100 Most Influential People." Adi Ignatius, editor-in-chief of the *Harvard Business Review*, said, "Meeting Jack Ma, you might be forgiven for thinking he's still an English teacher. The Chinese Internet entrepreneur is soft-spoken and elf-like—and he speaks really good English."

In 2014, Alibaba not only had the largest US-listed initial public offering, it was the largest global IPO in history. Jack Ma, the guy who failed the college entrance exam *twice*, raised $25 billion in stock sales for his company. Ma is an incredible example of what can happen when you commit to the single-minded pursuit of a Grand Vision and stick to your guns when the going gets tough. It just goes to show, with a Grand Vision and the will to succeed, the world is your oyster.

At the Alibaba.com annual shareholders meeting in 2009, Ma encouraged those in attendance to take matters into their own hands and take action in the form of starting businesses to cope with the economic downturn rather than waiting for government to help them. He reminded everyone that the great fortunes of the world were made by people who saw opportunities where others only saw problems.

In 2010, Ma was selected by *Forbes Asia* as one of Asia's Heroes of Philanthropy for his contribution to disaster relief and poverty. Regarding the future of Alibaba, he has said, "Our challenge is to help more people to make healthy money, 'sustainable money,' money that is not only good for themselves, but also good for the society. That's the transformation we are aiming to make."

William Henry "Bill" Gates (1955–)

Cofounder of Microsoft Corporation and Bill and Melinda Gates Foundation, world's richest man (2013)

"I really had a lot of dreams when I was a kid, and I think a great deal of that grew out of the fact that I had a chance to read a lot."

Bill grew up in a family that encouraged competition. There was always a reward for winning and a penalty for losing. He was a voracious reader as a child. Bill was feisty and at times combative.

He did well in school, but he was bored. His parents worried he might become a loner. Then at age thirteen, he began to show an interest in computer programming. At one point, he and his best friend, Paul Allen, had their school computer privileges revoked for hacking the computer to obtain free time on it. They were ultimately allowed back in the computer lab after they offered to debug the program they had hacked. Gates later developed a payroll program for the computer company they had hacked and a scheduling program for the school.

Gates and Allen, through hard work and perseverance, were unbelievably successful. He states, "I never took a day off in my twenties. . . . Not one."

A technology visionary and business trailblazer, Gates has said, "When Paul Allen and I started Microsoft . . . we had big dreams about software . . . about the impact it could have. We talked about a computer on every desk and in every home."

Try to imagine how absolutely absurd this idea would have been when, in 1975, Xerox had just closed their computer division. The only small desktop computer available was an Altair. Bill Gates, Paul Allen, and Monte Davidoff, on January 2, 1975, announced Altair BASIC, the first computer language program for personal computers. He also said, "The Internet is becoming the town square for the global village of tomorrow." What a Grand Vision!

When Microsoft was founded in 1975, the idea of the personal computer was, according to many, on its way out the door. Despite the challenges, Gates and his fellow founders at Microsoft took a dying industry and revamped it into the most widely used and ubiquitous technologies of the late twentieth and early twenty-first centuries. Through technological innovation, keen business strategy, and aggressive business tactics, he built the world's largest software business and took Microsoft from thirteen employees (and not much revenue) in 1978 to a company that as of 2015 had global annual revenue of more than $86 billion and 128,000 employees worldwide.

Now, Gates has a new Grand Vision: "By the year 2035, there will be almost no poor countries left in the world." He goes on to say, "It is a myth that poor countries are doomed to stay poor." Gates is aiming to fulfill his Grand Vision through the Bill and Melinda Gates Foundation, and he is succeeding in large part by getting others to buy into his Grand Vision and join him in it, including investment guru and fellow billionaire Warren Buffett, who is strongly committed to the mission of the Gates Foundation. In fact, in the five years since Gates and Warren Buffett joined forces to pledge the donation of half of their net wealth to charity, 193 individuals have jumped on board to pledge or give more than half of their fortunes away in life or in death. Talk about a major impact![24]

Elon Musk (1971–)
Founder of PayPal, SpaceX, and Tesla Motors

"Well, I work a lot . . . I mean a lot."

Elon Musk is a South African-born Canadian American engineer, inventor, and billionaire. He grew up in South Africa and, according to his brother, Kimbal, Elon was a big reader. "He would go through two books a day." In his teens, Elon says, he read a mountain of philosophical and religious books. When asked if any book in particular gave him solace, he cites *The Hitchhiker's Guide to the Galaxy.*

"It taught me that the tough thing is figuring out what questions to ask, but that once you do that, the rest is really easy. . . . I came to the conclusion that we should aspire to increase the scope and scale of human consciousness in order to better understand what questions to ask. Really, the only thing that makes sense is to strive for greater collective enlightenment."

At age fifteen, Musk decided to move to the United States. His mother was born in Canada, which was close enough. He got a Canadian passport and arrived in Montreal with very little money and no home. He spent the next year working at menial jobs to support himself while studying at Queens University in Ontario. In 1992, he was able to move to the United States after receiving a scholarship from the University of Pennsylvania. He earned his bachelor of science degree in physics the next year but decided to continue his studies at the Wharton School of the University of Pennsylvania for one more year and obtained a bachelor of science degree in economics as well.

Musk made his first fortune as a cofounder of PayPal, which revolutionized payment systems on the Internet.

Musk's Grand Vision could best be summed up by his statement to the *Los Angeles Times* in 2003, in the beginning days of his groundbreaking work with space technology company SpaceX: "I like to be involved in things that change the world."[25] So far, he's managed to take that Grand Vision to places not even he could have imagined.

He went on to make SpaceX wildly successful, cofounded SolarCity, and founded Tesla Motors, which is revolutionizing the electric vehicle market and positively disrupting business as usual in the car industry. NASA is now using the SpaceX Dragon spacecraft to resupply the International Space Station. Solar-City is based on the Grand Vision that within twenty years solar power will be the primary source of electrical power. He is building the first distributed-energy network and recently announced solar-powered home batteries that have the potential to revolutionize the way our homes and lives are powered while providing tremendous economic and environmental benefits.

When asked on a TED Talk interview how he has accomplished so much innovation in so many fields, he responded,

> I do think there's a good framework for thinking. It is physics . . . the sort of first principles reasoning . . . Boil things down to their fundamental truths and reason up from there, as opposed to reasoning by analogy. Through most of our life, we get through life by reasoning by analogy, which essentially means copying what other people do with slight variations. And you have to do that. Otherwise, mentally, you wouldn't be able to get through the day. But when you want to do something new, you have to apply the physics approach. Physics is really figuring out how to discover new things that are counterintuitive . . . So I think that's an important thing to do. Also, really pay attention to negative feedback, and solicit it, particularly from friends. This may sound like simple advice, but hardly anyone does that, and it's incredibly helpful.

Musk recently stated his next Grand Vision: "Build a 'hyperloop' to carry people from San Francisco to Los Angeles in thirty-five minutes." I would not put it past him to accomplish this vision too.

David H. Murdock (1923–)

American rags-to-riches
billionaire
"To do the impossible,
you must see the invisible."

David H. Murdock, a remarkably
successful American billionaire, painted the above sentence
on the wall of one of his many businesses—and has lived his
life that way.

Murdock dropped out of high school in the ninth grade
and was drafted by the US Army during World War II.
Returning from the war, he was homeless and destitute.
Because of a chance encounter, he obtained a loan to buy
a small diner, which he ran relentlessly and turned around.
He sold it for a profit ten months later.

Through grit and determination, Murdock then built a
business in the real estate industry, and in 1978, he acquired
control of International Mining. By the 1980s, he had
become the largest shareholder in Occidental Petroleum by
selling the company his 18 percent interest in Iowa Beef.

Today, when Murdock speaks about his difficult childhood and lack of formal education, he casts it as an unin-
tended gift. He says that because he felt the need to
compensate, he read constantly. Like so many others of
exceptional success, he educated himself, setting up his

own study curriculum. He was never able to rest on his credentials. Today, he says with pride, "I now employ mostly people with far greater credentials than me."

Presently, Murdock (now ninety-one) has been fulfilling his latest Grand Vision to build a state-of-the-art biotechnology research center in North Carolina. He has personally spent some $500 million in recent years to construct the North Carolina Research Campus, a scientific center dedicated to his conviction that consuming the right variety of plants holds the promise of optimal health and maximal life span.

As of this writing, *Forbes* magazine ranks Murdoch (with a net worth of $11.8 billion as of September 2015) as the thirty-third-richest person in the *Forbes 400* list and seventy-seventh in the *Billionaires* list.[26]

The Power of Goals

"Your goals are the road maps that guide you and show you what is possible for your life. Goals help you channel your energy into action."

—Les Brown (author and motivational speaker)

As you contemplate your Grand Vision, it's also important to contemplate the immediate changes necessary to begin down that path. Anybody can wish for success, and most people do. What sets those who achieve their Grand Vision apart from those who don't is found in the Power of Goals. Futurist, author, lecturer, and filmmaker Joel A. Barker said, "Vision without action is merely a dream. Action without vision just passes the time. Vision with action can change the world."

By its nature, a Grand Vision cannot be fulfilled overnight. It requires a specific strategy, careful planning, and then tenacious execution. Once you have thought through a strategy, creating specific goals that will serve as milestones to your Grand Vision is the catalyst that turns dreams into reality.

Written Goals

As with a Grand Vision, the only truly effective goals are those that are written down and continually reviewed. In writing a goal, make certain you're clear and your goal statement is simple and precise. A lack of clear intention is high on the list of causes for failure to achieve goals.

A fascinating study was conducted on the 1979 Harvard MBA class, where graduate students were asked about goal-setting. One of the questions was, "Have you set clear, written goals for your future and made plans to accomplish them?" The survey showed that only 3 percent had written goals and plans; 13 percent had goals, but they weren't in writing; and 84 percent had no goals at all.

Ten years later, the same group was interviewed again, and the result was incredibility telling. The 13 percent of the class who had goals but did not write them down was earning twice the amount of the 84 percent who had no goals. The 3 percent who had written goals were earning, on average, ten times as much as the other 97 percent of the class combined![27] While this study only looked at earnings to quantify success, I find it to be a great example of why creating clear and measurable goals and writing them down is a key to success. Feeling motivated?

Many people will not commit goals to writing because of the fear of failure. They fear a sense of shame would accompany failure to achieve a clearly defined goal. And that may be true for some people, though it ought not be. There is no shame in failing to reach a goal, only in failing to reach for it. Don't let fear hold you back.

Understand that "I want to be wealthy" is not a goal. It may be a wish, but it's not a goal. "If you find you can't measure it, rate it, or describe it, you probably can forget it as a goal," says Dr. Michael LeBoeuf, author of *Working Smart*.[28]

While I was in the Air Force, a fellow airman gave me a well-worn copy of *Think and Grow Rich* by Napoleon Hill, a book that profoundly changed my thinking and worldview.

I found the following passage startling: ". . . wishing will not bring riches. But desiring riches with a state of mind that becomes an obsession, then planning definite ways and means to acquire riches, and backing those plans with persistence which does not recognize failure, will bring riches."[29]

After reading this passage—at age eighteen, with no money and three more years to go on my judge-imposed tour of duty—I declared my first Grand Goal:

"By the time I am forty, I will be a millionaire."

I wrote this goal on a slip of paper and carried it in my wallet. I repeated it daily for years. In the chapter titled The Power of Rational Thinking, you will find how that first goal worked out.

Now, begin by writing your Grand Goal—your long-term vision converted to an audacious success goal. It is imperative the goal be clear, measurable, and time-sensitive. Put it in the form of a declarative statement. Here are some examples of clear, measurable, time-sensitive Grand Goals:

- I will write a book that will be on the *New York Times* best-seller list by December 2018.

- By age forty-five, I will be an ordained minister in the Presbyterian Church.

- I will become president of the company I am employed at before age fifty.

- I will be promoted to full colonel within five years from today.

Next, break your Grand Goal into shorter-term goals. These are controllable, measurable accomplishments, which will power you to your Grand Goal. An example of a goal in my case was, "I will get an education consisting of the knowledge necessary to help me become a successful real estate investor."

I have always believed in keeping your goals to yourself. Entrepreneur Derek Sivers, who created CD Baby in 1998 and sold it ten years later for $22 million, argues you should keep your goals a secret.

"Tests done since 1933 show that people who talk about their intentions are less likely to make them happen," he says. "Announcing your plans to others satisfies your self-identity just enough that you're less motivated to do the hard work needed."[30]

I also realized that achieving my Grand Goal would require sacrifice and risk, so I set another intermediate goal to save for the cost of obtaining an education. When I got my first job out of college, Joan and I set a new goal to start building our investment nest egg by saving 10 percent or more of everything we earned. It was hard to do, but we stuck with it because we had passion and enthusiasm for our Grand Goal.

Ladders to Success

No single path to success exists. Instead, you will have to travel many paths before you reach the top. To visualize what I mean, imagine a success tower surrounded by ladders, but you're unable to see above the first rung on any ladder. Take the ladder nearest at hand and climb the first rung. Then take your second step. If you find you're on a ladder of only three steps, you may need to change ladders and climb an adjacent ladder that offers more rungs. However, if that second ladder stops with only six rungs, you can then climb over to yet another ladder, which leads you still higher. No one job holds your complete future. Jobs are the rungs on a ladder, and the rungs never move. The future always lies in the person who holds the job. Each time you change ladders, you are reinventing yourself.

In my case, in order to reach my college goal, I set a short-term objective of getting a job to fund my living expenses and college tuition. My new job was in food service at the university I was attending. It paid $1.25 an hour and all I could eat. That job was like the bottom rung on a success ladder. I then became a student manager of the dining hall, the second rung on the food-service success ladder. Next, I became the student manager of the athletic dining facilities and received a full scholarship. This was my third success ladder. Finally, the head coach of the football team offered me the job of assistant manager of a fast-food franchise he had purchased. His brother-in-law was the manager and this new opportunity gave me a way to earn more and learn more.

After college, my next goal was to get a job with great potential. After several interviews, I was offered a job with United Parcel Service (UPS), where I was to help manage the company's vast real estate portfolio. This was the first rung on the UPS success ladder. We moved to Chicago and for the first three months, I was assigned to learn the philosophy and work ethic of this great company.

UPS was founded in 1907 by a sixth-grade dropout named Jim Casey, who was an autodidact and true genius. His wisdom and common sense were legendary. He had a simple belief that if you do your best and go the extra mile to satisfy the customer, the company and its people will prosper.

The Extra Mile

Always go the extra mile, because only a few people do, and the extra mile is where opportunity resides. Be early and stay late. Make the extra phone call. Do the extra research. Every time you do something, think of one more extra thing you can add. That will make you stand out from others and, over time, can make you incredibly successful.

A year after I joined UPS, I moved up the success ladder and was promoted to the headquarters in New York City. Everyone there was senior to me. In fact, I was an outsider and a threat to the other staff, many of whom had been with the company for years.

I knew that to move on up the UPS success ladder, I needed to outwork my peers. I made it a point to arrive at work earlier than anyone else and be the last to leave. No job was too small or too difficult for me. Every day, I made written commitments to myself. The following day, I reviewed those commitments and then made new ones. Within eighteen months, I was made the real estate manager for the largest region in the company. This was a big step up the UPS success ladder. When the company expanded service into the remaining nine US states, I was put in charge of the facilities task force, another step up the success ladder. When UPS decided to expand internationally, I was again put in charge of the effort to locate and set up new facilities across Germany. By age thirty, I was the youngest manager in UPS to be invited into the senior management incentive plan for the top one hundred employees. This represented the highest step on the UPS success ladder.

This is a great illustration of how the power of written commitments, especially on a day-to-day basis, can help you achieve your goals. I no longer write out my goals for each day, mostly because my goals and circumstances have changed, but I still aim to always provide far more than is expected of me every single day. It's that commitment to excellence that has allowed me to serve in many of the places I've served. I've carried that same attitude, going above and beyond without seeking recognition or fanfare. For many years we have tried to go the extra mile within our community, and I have always made a point of staying away from seeking recognition for the family name and instead putting my attention into the next goal to be accomplished.

My next step toward achieving my Grand Goal was to establish my own real estate investment company. In 1978, the national economy was beginning to recover from a severe recession. Many real estate developers had gone out of business. Banks had foreclosed on thousands of properties and were beginning to sell off some of those assets to rebuild their capital.

Joan and I decided it was time for me to start my own business. Because we had been saving 10 to 15 percent of everything we earned, we had enough to start our own company and support our family for at least three years. We took a risk, but our careful preparation and goal setting, along with our faithful execution of those goals, made it a relatively safe risk.

I began by conducting a national study to determine which city in the United States would be the best to start our new business. My study indicated that Charlotte, North Carolina, had the best future. I had been there only once before, when I unsuccessfully interviewed for a job in 1969. I commuted between Connecticut and Charlotte for several months in order to study the region in detail. Ultimately that research led me to identify what seemed to be an excellent investment opportunity. The lender and owner of the property, I discovered, was ready to unload assets, and my research indicated the market was beginning to come back. Thus began my entrepreneurial success, which has taken me far beyond the Grand Vision and the Grand Goals I wrote down many years ago.

In the years since leaving UPS, the *extra-mile* philosophy of company founder Jim Casey shaped a large portion of my success because it provided the organizing principle behind my travels up many success ladders.

The average guy is average for a reason, and the exceptional person is exceptional for a reason. Exceptional people simply do and provide more and give more than is expected. You've heard the saying "under promise and over deliver." I think my philosophy boils down to something even simpler: always keep your word, and always provide your customers, clients, etc., with your absolute best. Those two principles will carry you a long way.

Most people can do 100 percent of their job, but the people who give 110 percent or even 120 percent completing a job will excel further and faster. Always endeavor to stand out from the crowd by doing more than what is expected of you. This is harder to do, which is why most people can't or won't do it.

For example, in my real estate business, I always made sure to give my tenants more than they expected for their rent. I found that by providing extra services—like business improvement and outside retail consultants to help improve sales—I was able to retain business and develop loyal relationships that benefited both parties. By going above and beyond to improve our relationship with our tenants, we were able to ensure long-term success.

The Power of Knowledge

"Human behavior flows from three main sources: desire, emotion, and knowledge."

—Plato

When I was a child, my stepfather told me, "Stop asking questions. Remember, curiosity killed the cat." This message, told to countless children, is simply wrong. In reality, genius comes from the desire to know the what and how, and the why and where of everything—the unquenchable thirst to know the unknown. All achievements have their beginning in an idea, and all ideas are born of curiosity—the insatiable desire to learn. Those who seem to always be seeking to know why things are as they are rather than just accepting without question are naturals at this concept. But many of us need to better develop this curiosity.

Also, most children seem to ask a series of whys. It would start with a "Why?" And then when the adult gave an answer the child would respond again, "Why?" Finally, the adult would get tired and say, "Stop with the whys." It turns out those childlike instincts were correct. Indeed, asking the fundamental question *Why?* is an integral part of sophisticated process improvement programs like Six Sigma, which teaches that to get to the bottom of any problem you need to use the Five Whys technique, digging at least five levels deep into a problem with new "Why?" questions. The following is an example of the Five Whys technique:

Problem: You are on your way to work and your car stops in the middle of the road.

1. Why did your car stop? Because it ran out of gas.

2. Why did it run out of gas? Because I didn't buy any gas this morning.

3. Why didn't you buy any gas this morning? Because I didn't have any money.

4. Why didn't you have any money? Because I spent the last of my money on beer and a pack of cigarettes.

5. Why did you spend the last of your money on beer and cigarettes? Because I love beer and cigarettes.

As you can see, the fifth and final "Why?" leads you to a statement that you can take action upon.

Arnold Edinborough, a university professor and author, said, "Curiosity is the very basis of education, and if you tell me that curiosity killed the cat, I say the cat died nobly." Where would we be if people such as Christopher Columbus, Marie Curie, Michael Faraday, Thomas Edison, and so many others had lacked curiosity?

Curiosity is important because it allows us to move beyond our basic limitations and to see beyond our immediate, personal concerns. In short, knowledge is power. It exposes us to other perspectives and broadens narrow horizons, allowing us to see destinations we couldn't see before.

Knowledge can also increase our ability to empathize with and understand others, which is one of the most valuable traits you can have when it comes to accomplishing your goals.

Knowledge is a compounding asset. The more you learn, the easier it becomes to learn even more. So, rather than growing slowly, a dedication to learning will result in the exponential growth of knowledge. In fact, according to the *American Educator*, "Learning new things is actually a seamless process, but in order to study it and understand it better, cognitive scientists have approached it as a three-stage process—as you first take in new information (via observing, doing, listening, or reading), as you think about this information, and as the material is stored in memory."

Experts don't just know more than novices; they actually see problems differently. For many problems, the expert does not *need* to reason, but rather, can rely on memory of prior solutions. Indeed, in some domains, knowledge is much more important than reasoning or problem-solving abilities. For example, most of the differences among top chess players appear to be in how many game positions they know, rather than in how effective they are in searching for a good move.[31]

Learning and Adapting

The latest brain research seems to differentiate people based on the concept of whether they think their mind is either a) an evolving organism capable of growing and improving, or b) a fixed and unchanging organ. Those people who have a growth mindset and believe their mind can be improved through effort are typically more successful than those with a fixed mindset, who believe they are born with a certain amount of intelligence and talent and that nothing can or will change it.

In fact, Dr. Carol Dweck, researcher and author of *Mindset: The New Psychology of Success*, has proven that when people learn how the brain changes and grows in response to challenges, they're much more likely to persevere when they fail, since they don't believe that failure is a permanent condition. Dr. Dweck states, "People with a growth mindset see their qualities as things that can be developed through dedication and effort. They understand that no one has ever accomplished great things without years of passionate practice and learning."[32]

To that I would add, "and failing." You need to know that you are an evolving person, and that as such you have far more capacity to learn and improve than you can imagine. I have experienced so many failures along the way it is impossible to count them, but each time I have forgiven myself and tried to learn and keep moving up my ladders. Over the years some of my real estate investment projects did not work after months or even years of efforts and lots of money. One piece of land I invested in with the conviction that it would be ready for development within five years was not ripe for a project for twenty years.

Many times I hired people I thought were going to be great, only to discover they were just not a good fit. In other cases, I decided against hiring people who turned out to be quite successful elsewhere. That did not discourage me from hiring more people. It just taught me to be more thorough in my research of potential employees.

Fortunately, more of my ideas and projects succeeded than failed.

For thousands of years, all accumulated knowledge was contained in books that were mostly located in private libraries and then later in public libraries. Access to knowledge was therefore restricted by physical access to a building. This gave the leaders in societies most of the access to education and therefore most of the opportunity for further success. The learned class was limited to a very few in each society.

We are just now beginning to comprehend the power of free and accessible knowledge. Today, we have more information in our pockets than all of the ancient libraries of the world combined. This information revolution has fundamentally changed large portions of daily life for people around the world, making it easier than ever for curious individuals to gain access to knowledge they could not have dreamed of accessing in years past.

It is critical to remember that easy access to information does not make gaining knowledge easy. You still must take the initiative and put forth the effort to learn the skills and information you will need, tailored to your specific goals. In his book *Information Systems Development: Methodologies, Techniques, and Tools*, Guy Fitzgerald says on the information explosion, "Managing and applying knowledge is not the same as accessing information. The sheer quantity and diversity of information now available at the touch of a button can as easily overwhelm and disable as it can liberate and enable. It is not access to information that counts, but what we access, how and why, how we engage critically with it. To do this we have to learn how to build our confidence in using different resources."[33]

When I set my first Grand Vision and Grand Goal, I also set an objective of gaining the appropriate knowledge necessary to fulfill each of them. Because I had not graduated from high school, my educational path was somewhat unconventional.

I had earned a GED certificate and a number of college credits by taking equivalency examinations and courses while in the Air Force. After completing military service, I enrolled in college to acquire the necessary knowledge for financial success. I knew my path to success would reflect my family's legacy of making wealth from the land. At the time, only four colleges in the country offered a major in real estate.

Since I was working full time to pay for college, I had little interest in subjects not related to my ambition. Every course I took was aimed at learning a specific skill or knowledge needed to achieve my Grand Goal of becoming a millionaire by age forty. Therefore, I designed my own college curriculum. I took psychology courses in order to better understand myself. I studied logic and philosophy in order to develop better thinking skills, and sales, speech, and debate classes to be able to sell my ideas to others. Since business is held together by legal principles, I took several law courses in order to know how to protect my business deals and myself. Courses in real estate, geology, and geography were absolutely necessary since that was to be the core of my path to wealth and success. And I took history courses because I found them fascinating and nothing is really new anyway.

In addition to university courses, I read dozens of leadership and self-help books like this one, such as *How to Win Friends & Influence People*, *The Power of Positive Thinking*,[34] and so many others. It turns out that my self-designed study curriculum worked well for me. The formal education phase was just the beginning of a lifetime of continuous learning and honing of the skills and habits necessary for an exceptional life of success.

What are the specific areas of knowledge or skills you will need to acquire on your journey toward success? You might gain knowledge from the biographies of others who have already been successful in your area of interest. Could you improve your negotiating skills? How about your ability to speak clearly and convincingly?

They say "knowledge is power," but that's not quite right. The true Power of Knowledge is only unlocked by those who put their knowledge to practical use. I strongly recommend against seeking college degrees in concentrations not directly associated with your Grand Vision and Grand Goals.

Success requires an ability to consider facts, weigh arguments, and make decisions in the best interest of fulfilling your Grand Vision, regardless of your personal and emotional connections to whatever quandary you face.

Rational vs. Emotional Thinking

Rational or logical thinking is the unemotional, objective approach to decision making. Thinking logically is thinking with your right brain and is based on what you *know* is right. Math is a good example of logical thinking.

If you've read any of Sir Arthur Conan Doyle's books about Sherlock Holmes, the concept of rational thinking will be clear. Sherlock's insights in the field of crime solving are based on facts, rather than on emotion or preconceived notions. Put another way, "just the facts" boiled down to "elementary, my dear Watson." All people are capable of rational thinking.

In the many books of the Temperance Brennan series, upon which the TV series *Bones* is based, novelist and forensic anthropologist Kathy Reichs presents a protagonist who is an extremely rational thinker. In fact, Brennan cannot understand others around her who operate on a more emotional level. Her lack of social skills provides most of the humor in the books and the show, while her ability to stay focused strictly on the facts solves the case. I have met Kathy and her writings are true to her personality. She is a very charming and rational thinker.

Emotional thinking, also known as thinking with your left brain, is based on what you *feel* is right. It is more of a creative way of thinking, having to do with your imagination and how differently you can see things.

That is not to say emotional thinking is bad. Where would we be without love, compassion, or joy? All of these are emotions, but so are anger, greed, and lust.

The one emotion that will torpedo your long-term goals and aspirations, though, is impulsiveness, the temptation to grab immediate gratification, as opposed to delaying gratification in pursuit of your longer-term goals. Impulse control is simply discipline coupled with perseverance.

I am more of a rational thinker and find it necessary to constantly work to modify my instinct toward rationality.

I mentioned earlier that when I started working at UPS, Joan and I decided we would save at minimum 10 percent off the top of each paycheck to begin building our nest egg; we made a commitment to live *below* our means. While our friends were buying new cars and taking exotic vacations, we kept our older car, and for our vacations, we went to Joan's parents' house to mooch for a couple of weeks. (Her mother was a great cook!) This behavior has since been called delayed gratification. We called it growing the Golden Goose, which in turn would produce golden eggs. For nine years, we saved, invested, and deferred most luxuries.

At age thirty-four, we had saved enough to start my own business in real estate development and investment. Within four years, at thirty-eight, I had achieved my first Grand Goal to be a millionaire by age forty.

The realization made for a wonderful moment, but soon after I felt like I had an empty spot in my psyche. So then I set this goal:

"I will have a net worth of $10 million by age fifty."

Having achieved that goal by age forty-five, I had reached my definition of financial independence.

Your success in achieving your goals will be dependent on the ability to manage decisions by understanding when to use your emotions for good, and when to rely on rational, logical thinking. This has a lot to do with controlling your impulses for your greater goals. When your impulse of the moment might or will get in the way of your greater goal, you must let your rational logical thinking take over. By example, you are tempted to take the day off to go to a ball game when you know you should be focused on working toward your goal. Self-awareness and self-discipline are critical here. Overcome your desire for what you know is short-term gratification for the benefit of your longer-term goals.

Beware of Rationalized Thinking

There is a huge difference between rational thinking and *rationalized* thinking. Rationalized thinking is when you use impulse and self-gratification to make a decision and then come up with the rationalized reasons to support the decision you've already made.

For example, you see a shiny new car and immediately want it. Unfortunately, it is beyond your means. In addition, you have three children and a wife, and no savings. First, you think, "I will look great," and then, "It is more reliable than my current car," followed by, "My neighbors will be jealous, and it gets better gas mileage than the old one."

The salesperson then seals the deal by telling you the six-year loan will be at almost no interest. Rationalized thinking just got the best of you.

Rational thinking, on the other hand, is the exact opposite of rationalized thinking. Rational thinking is the ability to make a decision based purely on a clearheaded analysis of the facts. To go back to the car example, this would mean forgoing that shiny new car. Not only forgoing the shiny new car but researching your options for affordable cars, realistically assessing your financial ability to buy a car (and what options fit into your budget), and calculating not just your current but your future ability to pay for the vehicle as well.

Not only is this a far more helpful way to conduct your life and your business, it will leave you far better positioned for long-term success because you will avoid irresponsible decisions and instead make choices that benefit you and those around you.

FAITH *is like*
the WIND —
You can't SEE *it,*
but you KNOW
it's there.

The Power of Faith

There are things we cannot see, know, or understand, and in order to be successful, we must come to terms with, and even embrace, that inability.

Faith is the belief that there are supernatural powers that surpass all human understanding and that dominate or strongly influence the fate of human beings. The creator of all is called a thousand different names around the world. The Bible says in Hebrews 11, "By faith, we understand that the universe was formed at God's command, so that what is seen was not made out of what is visible." The various religions of the world are man's creations in an attempt to bring order and reason to this basic faith. To have faith is to gain the knowledge of forgiveness and the understanding that we will all fall short of perfection. The Prophet Muhammad said, "You will not enter paradise until you have faith. And you will not complete your faith until you love one another."

When you believe there is a power greater than the universe itself and that power transcends all human rules and regulations, biases, prejudices, manipulations, or failings, you also receive the gift of prayer—an open channel for one-on-one conversation with the creator of all.

Most people let their present moments slip through their fingers, half-lived. They avoid the present by worrying about the future or living in the past. They forget that they are creatures who are subject to the limitations of time and space. What they also do not realize is that their creator walks with them only in the present.

Nothing in life is random. As you give yourself more and more to a life of constant communion with the creator, you will find that you simply have no time for worry. Thus, you are freed to let faith's spirit direct your steps. George Washington, America's first president, said, "It is impossible to account for the creation of the universe without the agency of a Supreme Being."

As I have traveled the world, I have observed that if you mention any specific religious group, you will please some and offend others. True faith transcends all and is beyond any sectarianism or selfishness.

A few years ago, I was honored to hear Dr. Francis Collins speak at the National Prayer Breakfast. Dr. Collins headed the Human Genome Project charged with mapping the human DNA code. He led two thousand scientists from six continents in the shared task of decoding and transliterating the three billion letters that make up the human genome. He said, "From my perspective . . . the scientific and religious worldviews are not only compatible but also inherently complementary." He spoke of faith in a personal way.

Through faith, we are provided with reservoirs of strength, tenacity, judgment, fairness, and discipline necessary for our success.

The Power of Persistence

"It is hard to beat a person who never gives up."
— Babe Ruth, the greatest player in
the history of baseball

Persistence, also known as determination or resilience, may be the most important Power necessary for any form of success.

Justin Sachs, a hugely successful author and entrepreneur, writes in his book *The Power of Persistence*,

The truth is that persistence equals success. What I mean by that is, if we look at those who are the most successful in the world, persistence is the most common denominator. Persistence is the thing that we've seen in each and every individual who has created the most successful businesses, political careers, relationships, etc. Those that are losing the most weight—Persistence. Those that stop smoking—Persistence. Everywhere we look, we see signs of persistence in those that are creating the most challenging and rewarding results. It is not always natural, it's a learned trait. What this means, though, is that success is simply a choice.[35]

Thomas Edison's teacher told his mother her son was "too stupid to learn anything." The same teacher called him a "dolt" and asked Edison's mother to take him home to teach him. It is said that after his mother read the note from his teacher, she called Thomas to her and said that his teacher told her that he was gifted and would benefit more from being home schooled. Later, he was fired from his first two jobs for not being productive enough. Even as an inventor, Edison kept failing. He made thousands of unsuccessful attempts at perfecting the light bulb. Of course, all those unsuccessful attempts finally resulted in the design that worked. When he succeeded, he said, "Our greatest weakness lies in giving up. The most certain way to succeed is always to try just one more time."

Willpower

The driving force behind persistence is willpower, which is defined as the ability to control your attention, impulses, emotions, and desires in order to do something even though it is more difficult and uncomfortable than you thought.

Most people struggle with their own willpower issues, whether it is about food, weight, alcohol, tobacco, or even criminal activity. According to the American Psychological Association, people name the lack of willpower as the number one reason they struggle to meet their goals.[38] You must be different.

You can catch self-control from good role models. This is one of several reasons why friends and mentors are vitally important to your success. So choose your friends intentionally and carefully. But beware: you can also catch the urge to spend money you don't have, eat or drink too much, or stay out too late, as well as many other bad habits you've picked up from friends.

The best summary of how willpower and desire combined are an unbeatable force for success was presented by Napoleon Hill in his book *Think and Grow Rich* in 1937, at the height of America's Great Depression. He wrote, "Willpower and desire, when properly combined, make an irresistible pair. There is no substitute for persistence! It cannot be supplanted by any other quality! Remember this and it will hearten you, in the beginning, when the going may seem difficult and slow. Those who have cultivated the habit of persistence seem to enjoy insurance against failure."[38] I have had many employees over the years who exhibited strong willpower but were short on the burning desire to be exceptional. Think about members of the military who can accomplish powerful acts of self-discipline and willpower. But few go on to greatness. The missing ingredient is the unquenchable desire to accomplish exceptional goals.

Willpower and stubbornness are not the same thing. The former breeds perseverance that leads to success, while the latter breeds pride and confrontation that hinders it. I would define stubbornness (an inherently negative trait) as the inflexible, unbending commitment to an attitude or position, despite evidence or advice to the contrary.

A big part of success is having the humility and grace to acknowledge when you're wrong, and the courage and freedom to pivot or change direction in the pursuit of your goals. Willpower is inherently a positive trait, as the drive to succeed or persevere despite the obstacles—whether the obstacle is the collapse of the financial system or your body screaming at you to stop running the last lap. In other words, stubbornness will kill your dream, but your dream can't survive for long without willpower.

A great example of the tremendous value of willpower in my own life was when I stopped smoking. As I mentioned earlier, I started smoking when I was nine years old. When I was thirty-three (and still smoking), Joan became pregnant with our second daughter, Melissa Joan, who came to be known as Missy. I was smoking one of my many cigars for the day when the nurse came out and informed me that I had a new daughter, and that Joan and Missy were doing fine.

I was overjoyed to have another daughter in our family, and right then and there, I extinguished the stub of my cigar and committed to quitting smoking, after twenty-four years. I said, "This is my gift to my family. I hereby quit smoking." And quit smoking I did. Once that decision was made, for me there was no going back on that commitment.

While that decision was completely spontaneous, I also think it was highly intuitive. Smoking was becoming a more well-known health issue, but the public was not made as aware of it as they are today.

So while I knew that smoking certainly wasn't good for me, I simply decided that for my new daughter and the rest of my family, I should commit to quitting.

By making the cessation of my smoking habit a gift to my child, I was able to motivate myself in a uniquely powerful way, which I found highly useful and effective for other difficult and challenging goals later in life, as well.

If you make a commitment to yourself, you can disappoint yourself, and it will not be a big deal. To put this another way, it's easy to rationalize your own failures when you're only letting yourself down. But if you make a commitment to someone you love, most people can't imagine failing to follow through on that commitment. I succeeded in large part because I didn't give myself any wiggle room for cheating or relapsing. Does this mean that I wasn't tempted to smoke ever again? As with nearly any difficult challenge, that was absolutely not the case. There were many days and moments when I was tempted to give in to my impulses, especially when I was under stress or in social situations where it would have been normal or acceptable.

Whenever that temptation occurred, however, I reminded myself that I would be taking a gift back, and that's how I persuaded myself to stick to it. It all goes back to basic self-discipline.

This demonstrates one of the basic problems of success, which is that most people are unsuccessful because they can't control their impulses.

One of my favorite examples of the impulse problem comes from the animal kingdom. White-tailed deer, which are abundant in my home state of North Carolina, are logical, wary animals most of the year, except for their breeding season, usually referred to as the "rut" by hunters. Sometime in mid-to-late fall, these deer get overly excited and turn into complete idiots.

They pose a huge risk to motorists during this season because they run out in front of cars and they also ignore the warning signs that a hunter may be nearby and meet an untimely end, all because of a hormone-driven impulse. You probably know of people who become impulsive and hormone driven by others of the opposite sex and lose rational control with disastrous consequences to their loved ones and themselves. If asked, you can probably name dozens of people in the news who have lost everything dear to them for this simple reason.

Willpower is your ability to know that emotion and compulsion can be dangerous and that rational thought of consequences, if allowed to rule, can save you from potential disaster.

Procrastination Is the Best Friend of Failure

A sense of urgency is vital to persistence. The best way to get anything done is to begin immediately and practice a sense of urgency. This is known as the Power of Now. Successful people do it now. Always be willing to make decisions. It is the most important quality in good leaders. They know that otherwise they could fall victim to the Law of Diminishing Intent, which states, "The longer you wait to do something, the greater the chances are you'll never do it." It is extremely important for you to take the initial step—now.

In the case of setting goals for your Grand Vision, it means write them down as soon as they are clear in your mind. You might think you'll remember, but odds are you won't. Think of writing it down as the first step in taking action. Now you will need to plan the next step. Make it an easy one that you know you can do. An example could be that you will commit to yourself to read something motivational for one hour each day or that you will get up an hour earlier each day for the next week and work on your list of what it will take for you to move to the next level on your ladders to success. That will give you the confidence to take the next step. Keep going, and before you know it you will reach your goal.

In order to be persistent, you must first fail; otherwise, there is no need to persist. You will never be good at something unless you are bad at it first. I've learned to embrace failure—own it, learn from it, and take full responsibility for making sure I don't repeat it. Walt Disney was turned down by banks and investors 302 times before he secured financing for his dream of creating "the Happiest Place on Earth." Today, because of his persistence, millions of people have been able to enjoy his Disney theme parks.

You—yes, you—have already demonstrated amazing persistence in your life. When you were a baby, you tried to stand up and failed many times before you finally were able to stand. When you tried to walk, you failed many times. As you failed, you persisted and persisted, learning from each failure until you made the necessary changes to succeed. The same is true when you tried to run, speak, and dance. We are born with deep-seated persistence, and some people maintain the trait the remainder of their lives. Others learn at some point that it might be easier to just give up. Therein lies the difference between success and failure.

Many of history's most successful people faced seemingly impossible obstacles along their way. The following pages contain the stories of some men and women who understood the Power of Perseverance, and wielded it well in their personal quest for success.

George Washington (1732–1799)
First president of the United States of America
"99 percent of failures come from people who make excuses."

The founding father of the United States of America, George Washington, had a rough upbringing. Although his father and two older half-brothers were educated in England, a lack of money prevented him from studying abroad. Unlike many of the founding fathers, Washington did not attend college, but he did begin the lifelong pursuit of self-education. He was an avid reader and studied a variety of subjects ranging from military arts to agriculture. He didn't get along with his mother. This lack of affection during his childhood led him to be aloof and reticent in adulthood.

George Washington ran for a seat in the Virginia House of Burgesses in 1755—and lost. He ran again in 1758 and won. He remained in the House of Burgesses until 1775. During his tenure, Washington was not outspoken, nor did he introduce any innovative legislation. In 1759, he married Martha Custis, a wealthy, young widow from Virginia.

Washington wasn't a particularly good military strategist or tactician. He lost more battles than he won throughout his military career. The Battles of Fort Necessity, Monongahela, Long Island, White Plains, Brandywine, Fort Washington, and Germantown were all battles where Washington's forces were defeated. Despite this roster of defeats, Washington brought many important characteristics to his military command. What made Washington a great leader, though, was his vision and persistence. Setbacks, defeat, betrayal, and failure would not deter him. Even when it seemed that all was lost, he persisted.

George Washington is the only president in United States history to have been *unanimously* elected, twice. He oversaw the creation of a strong national government that suppressed a rebellion and pioneered many innovations in governance that persist to this day, including using a Cabinet system. The peaceful transition from his presidency to that of John Adams established a tradition that continues as a model for democracy today. Washington was the leader of the first successful revolution against a colonial empire in world history. Think about that. Washington was and always will be the father of his country. At his death, Washington was eulogized as "first in war, first in peace, and first in the hearts of his countrymen."

Abraham Lincoln (1809–1865)
Sixteenth president of the
United States
"Adhere to your purpose, and you
will soon feel as well as you ever
did. On the contrary, if you falter
and give up, you will lose the power of
keeping any resolution, and will regret it all your life."

President Abraham Lincoln was one of the most persistent men in American history. Born into poverty in 1809, he and his family were forced out of their home when he was seven and he had to go to work. When Lincoln was only nine, his mother died. At age twenty-two, he failed in business. At twenty-three, he was defeated in his bid for election to the Illinois legislature and lost his job. At twenty-four, he suffered the death of his wife-to-be and soon after had a nervous breakdown. At twenty-eight, he was rejected in a marriage proposal. At twenty-nine, he was defeated for the position of speaker of the Illinois House of Representatives.

However, at age thirty-seven, he succeeded in being elected to the United States Congress and served only *one* term. At age forty-five, Lincoln ran for the United States Senate—and lost. Two years later, he vied to become vice president of the United States—and lost. Next, he again ran for the United States Senate—and lost. That was 1858. In 1860, he ran for president of the United States—and won.

Abraham Lincoln—with no formal education, no wealth, and the biography of a serial loser—became the sixteenth president of the United States. Thanks to his persistence, this man, who lacked connections, charisma, or even good looks, is considered by many scholars to have been the best president in United States history. He is credited with holding the country together by leading the Union to victory in the Civil War. His actions and beliefs led to the emancipation of African Americans from the bonds of slavery. More than fifteen thousand books have been written about President Lincoln—more books than have been written about any other person in world history, with the exception of Jesus Christ.

Nelson Mandela (1918–2013)

First black president of South Africa

"It always seems impossible until it's done."

Nelson Mandela was originally named Rolihlahla Mandela, which in his tribal language commonly translates as "troublemaker." Mandela's father lost both his tribal leader title and fortune over a dispute with the local colonial magistrate and they were forced to move to a village so small it didn't even have roads.

In school, he was told his new first name would be Nelson. When he was nine years old, his father died, and he was adopted by the chief of the Thembu people as a favor to his deceased father. Mandela moved to the chief's royal residence and was given the same status and responsibilities as the regent's two other children. From the time Mandela came under the guardianship of the chief, he was groomed to assume high office, not as a chief, but as a counselor to a chief.

Always a fighter for justice, Mandela was expelled from college in 1940 for leading a student strike, although he was later able to earn his undergraduate degree. He became active in the anti-apartheid movement, joining the African National Congress (ANC). For the next twenty years, Mandela directed peaceful, nonviolent acts of defiance against the South African government's racist policies. He also founded the law firm Mandela and Tambo, which provided free or low-cost legal counsel to unrepresented blacks. In 1956, Mandela and 150 others were arrested and charged with treason for their political advocacy. They were ultimately acquitted of the charges.

By 1961, Mandela began to believe that armed struggle was the only way to achieve change. He cofounded an armed offshoot of the ANC dedicated to sabotage and guerilla war tactics to end apartheid. He went on to organize a national workers strike and was arrested and sentenced to five years in prison. In 1963, Mandela was brought to trial again when he and ten others were sentenced to life imprisonment for political offenses, including sabotage.

While in prison, Mandela earned a bachelor of law degree through a University of London correspondence program. He was released from prison in 1990, eventually forgiving the jailers who had mistreated him and insisting on national unity in an intensely divided country.

In all, Mandela fought against racial segregation in South Africa for fifty-one years, twenty-seven of which were from a prison cell. Even from there, he was the most significant black leader in South Africa. On several occasions, he was offered his freedom in exchange for compromising his beliefs. He always refused.

For his beliefs, persistence, and sacrifice, Nelson Mandela received the Nobel Peace Prize in 1993. Then in 1994, he became the first black president of South Africa. He changed the course of history for millions of people around the world.

J. K. "Jo" Rowling (1965–)

Best-selling author
"I had an old typewriter and a big idea."

Joanne Rowling was a bright, young girl who wrote fantasy stories as a child to cope with a troubled home life. She took the entrance exams for Oxford University but was not accepted. She went on to the University of Exeter, where she was known as quietly competent.

Just seven years out of college, J. K. Rowling said about herself, "I am the biggest failure I know." Her marriage had failed, she was jobless and on welfare with her child, plus she was diagnosed with clinical depression. She later described her early failure this way:

> Failure meant a stripping away of the inessential. I stopped pretending to myself that I was anything other than what I was and began to direct all my energy to finishing the only work that mattered to me. Had I really succeeded at anything else, I might never have found the determination to succeed in the one area where I truly belonged. I was set free, because my greatest fear had been realized, and I was still alive, and I still had a daughter whom I adored, and so rock bottom became a solid foundation on which I rebuilt my life.[38]

After she completed her seminal masterpiece, *Harry Potter and the Philosopher's Stone*, it was rejected by twelve publishers before it was finally published. Her persistence, against overwhelming odds, finally paid off. Harry Potter is now a global brand worth billions of dollars. The last four Harry Potter books of the seven-book series are the fastest-selling books in history. These books have been credited with renewing an interest in reading among young people.

Sir James Dyson (1947–)
The world's first billionaire inventor

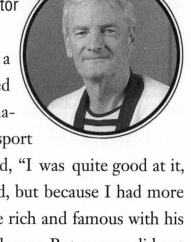

Early on, James Dyson became a long-distance runner. He claimed he learned the value of determination and persistence through this sport of solitary self-discipline. He said, "I was quite good at it, not because I was physically good, but because I had more determination." Sir James became rich and famous with his invention of the bagless vacuum cleaner. But success did not just happen. In the late 1970s, Dyson had the idea of using cyclonic separation to create a vacuum cleaner that would not lose suction as it picked up dirt. Partly supported by his wife's salary as an art teacher, and after five years of experimentation and 5,127 prototypes, he perfected his product. But then none of the leading vacuum manufacturers would make his product, so he set up his own manufacturing company. He almost went bankrupt several times. Dyson said that he learned the quality of determination that took him through these trials from long-distance running.

Dyson has since expanded his inventions to include the Dyson Airblade, a fast hand dryer. Dyson's most recent product is a fan without external blades, which he calls the Air Multiplier.

Dyson says, "A lot of people give up when the world seems to be against them, but that's the point when you should push a little harder. I use the analogy of running a race. It seems as though you can't carry on, but if you just get through the pain barrier, you'll see the end and be okay. Often, just around the corner is where the solution will happen."[39]

In 2002, Dyson set up a foundation to support design and engineering education. The foundation's aim is to inspire young people to become engineers by encouraging students to think differently and to make mistakes. The foundation also supports medical and scientific research in partnership with charities.

Mark Cuban (1958–)
American businessman and investor

Mark Cuban admits he did not do well in his early jobs. His parents wanted him to have a normal job, so he tried carpentry but hated it. He was a short-order cook but a bad one. He waited tables but couldn't even open a bottle of wine.

He applied lessons learned in his failures as he started Broadcast.com, an audio and video portal, which he later sold to Yahoo for $5.7 billion in stock. His failures also helped him succeed when he bought and turned around the Dallas Mavericks NBA franchise and cofounded HDNet, an all-high-definition television network. And these are just a few of his successful ventures that have landed him at number 144 on the *Forbes* 400 Richest Americans list, as well as a gig as a guest venture capitalist "shark" on ABC's *Shark Tank* reality TV show. In 2011, Cuban wrote an e-book, *How to Win at the Sport of Business: If I Can Do It, You Can Do It.* He states, "The beauty of success, whether it's finding the girl of your dreams, the right job, or financial success, is that it doesn't matter how many times you have failed, you only have to be right once . . . then everyone can tell you how lucky you are."[40]

I particularly enjoy his observation, "As I would learn later in life, money makes you extremely handsome."

The Power of Hard Focus

"Concentration is the secret of strength in politics, in war, in trade; in short, in all the management of human affairs. . . . The successful man is the average man, focused."

—Ralph Waldo Emerson

Hard focus is the ability to concentrate all your talents and attention on whatever is critical at that moment. For some people, hard focus comes naturally, but for most of us, it's an acquired trait. Without it, you cannot accomplish anything of great value. Hard focus is the Power that ties all the other Powers together.

Bill Clinton and I were playing golf when he shared with me what happened when he was playing a round of golf with the champion Jack Nicklaus the week before. Bill said, "When I won a hole, Jack didn't speak to me again for three holes." I asked if that hurt his feelings, and he replied, "No. I understood. He's a competitor, and losing a hole to me, an average golfer, shocked him back into hard focus. He was probably not even aware I was there."

In baseball, when you're at bat, when do you look at the bat? When throwing a football, when do you look at the ball? The answer is, you don't—you look at the target. The great batter Ted Williams could tell which way the ball was spinning when he was at bat. He had hard focus.

In 1999 and again in 2005, the US Open Golf Championship was to be played at Pinehurst, North Carolina. John Belk, patriarch of the Belk Department Store Chain and a dear friend and member of the US Open President's Council, invited me to join him to play the famous Pinehurst No. 2 course a few days before the tournament. Also playing both times was the famed University of North Carolina at Chapel Hill basketball coach Dean Smith and his successor, Roy Williams. John and I negotiated our handicaps and bet them twenty dollars on the first round. We lost. The next time we met, I said to John, "Let's renegotiate the number of strokes they will give us and bet twenty dollars again."

John said, "Just give them the money, because you don't get it. They're extremely competitive when it comes to sports. It really doesn't matter how many strokes they give us; they will win because they have more passion and hard focus to win at sports than we will ever have." After that, we played, and then paid up again. That's how I gained insight into the extreme power of hard focus.

Positive—Negative

By focusing on positive or negative thoughts, you can bring about positive or negative results. This belief is based on the idea that people and their thoughts are made from pure energy, plus the belief that like energy attracts like energy. Therefore, when you focus on the elements of success, you call all your Powers together for the accomplishment of your goal. Successful people know the importance of concentrating on one thing at a time. Lack of focus is often the reason for failure. When you are procrastinating, hesitating, and stopping, it is because you are concentrating on the ideas that take your focus away from your goal.

Likewise, when you focus on negative aspects of your situation, it serves as a double-edged sword of discouragement about your circumstances and a major roadblock to future action. It is difficult to motivate yourself to take that all-important first step toward success when you can only focus on the bad things that have happened or are happening to you.

On the other hand, developing positive thought patterns and then focusing them on accomplishing your goal can have an incredible impact. By focusing on the positive, you can impact positive change in your life and the lives of others. It is absolutely imperative that you develop a singular focus on your success and keep negative thoughts and attitudes (both your own and others) from polluting your focus.

This not only will make it easier and less intimidating to take that first step in a positive direction, but it will smooth the road to success and make it easier to navigate whatever challenges come your way. If you are tempted to a more pessimistic outlook on life, as many people are, I would encourage you to spend extra time focusing on the positive aspects of your road to success as a key part of accomplishing your goals. I believe that with just a little bit of positive focus, you can accomplish far beyond what you think you are capable of. I know I did.

The law of attraction is the concept that like attracts like. When you focus on the work at hand, you will start to attract thoughts about it that you can work on. Then those thoughts will attract more thoughts, and before you know it, you are in the flow. Each time you are distracted, continue to focus, and you will find yourself moving again.

Average people allow time to impose its will on them. Desiring success means you don't want to be average. Remarkable people impose their will on their time. By example, average people who are given two weeks to complete a task will instinctively adjust their effort so it takes two weeks to finish. Exceptional people are focused on Do It, Do It Right, and Do It Right Now.

I
believe
in GOOD
people

The Powers of Mentors and Friends

"Just about any personality trait or skill can be learned; simply find it in someone you know and copy it. Then watch what happens."

—Steve Goodier

I f you want a helping hand on your way through life, reach up to people you admire and respect. Do so even though it may be more comfortable to reach down to associate with people to whom you may feel superior. One of the easiest ways for this to happen is to allow a good friend to connect you with one of his or her good friends and so on. Luck plays a role in life, and there's no better way to increase your luck than by knowing as many good people as possible. A big contributor to success consists of time spent with people you respect, people who are willing to share their Powers with you. The Power of Mentors and Friends lies in the truth that you grow your own Power by seeking and sharing it with others. Your mentors do not need to be living, as you will read. You also don't need to spend much time with them. If you gain great insight by being in the presence of someone only briefly, that is enough.

Malcolm Gladwell states that genius is not the only, or even the most important, thing in determining success. In his book *Outliers*, he discusses the story of Christopher Langan. He began talking at six months and taught himself to read before age four. He grew up in poverty and was beaten by his stepfather until about fourteen, when he began weight training and threw his stepfather out of the house.

Langan has a colossal head with a circumference of twenty-five and one-half inches (XXXL) compared to the average adult male head circumference of less than twenty-two and one-half inches. His IQ is an incredible 195 (or one in a billion people). He has been a cowboy, bouncer, construction worker, and a Park Service firefighter. Gladwell thinks that he has not reached a high level of success because of the environment in which he grew up. With no leaders or mentors in Langan's life to help him take advantage of his exceptional gifts, he had to develop by himself. "No one—not rock stars, not professional athletes, not software billionaires, and not even geniuses—ever makes it alone," writes Gladwell.[41]

It is substantially more difficult to accomplish your goals without the feedback and guidance of those who are ahead of you in life. Mentors are a key part of your road to success. Whether it's perfecting your golf swing, or learning how to deal with difficult employees, cultivating the humility and eagerness to learn from and absorb the wisdom of your mentors is a key component of achieving mastery.

Life gives you a family, but you get to pick your friends—so, choose carefully. If you choose well, your friends and mentors are the people you can count on for honest advice, wisdom, and perspective. Think about the types of people you want to be with. Remember, *you* choose *them*. Inventory your current friends. Are they people you both respect and admire? Do they encourage you to want to be more? Do they have a generally positive attitude? Are they truthful and honest? Do they truly want you to be successful? Never spend time with people you do not trust. Nothing good can come from it. If the people around you make you unhappy, it's not their fault. They are in your life because you drew them to you—and you let them remain. Remember hardworking people like to be around hardworking people and kind people like to associate with kind people. Also, successful people are attracted to other successful people. But beware, losers are attracted to losers too.

When you meet someone new, treat him or her as a potential friend. Assume he or she is a winner and will become a positive force in your life. On occasion, you'll be disappointed, but your network will grow if you follow this path. Great friendships are a form of love, and who doesn't want more love in their life? There are times when someone will pass through your life and leave something of great value. Be on the lookout.

Stay alert, though: negative people emit negative thoughts, which are both toxic and contagious and they leave scars on your psyche. Avoid negative people, because negative thoughts drain you of energy and keep you from being in the present. The more you give in to your negative thoughts or the negative thoughts of others, the stronger they will become.

It's easy to dwell on your mistakes. When I get angry with myself for being critical of someone else's mistake, I try to make amends by asking them to forgive me for being short. It lightens the air and immediately improves my attitude. When I find I am having a negative day, I change it immediately by doing something unexpected and extraordinary for a stranger. For example, it is amazing medicine to give a clerk in a store or a server who normally does not receive tips a twenty-dollar bill.

Another thing I like to do when I am feeling down is to stop whatever I am doing and concentrate on five things I am truly grateful for in my life. Then I thank my Lord.

Resist the temptation to assume that a mentor must be more successful than you, older than you, or even alive at the same time as you. My first mentor was my grandfather, who died long before I was born. I grew up hearing the stories of his great success and was inspired to seek my own.

You'll be amazed who will be willing to share time with you if you ask them to join you for breakfast, lunch, coffee, a meeting—a place where they can share and you can listen. My mentors and friends have been extremely generous with their time. Add new people to your list and take others off as circumstances change. Make sure to contact each of your longer-term mentors at least once a month in some fashion—perhaps with a note, a photograph, a clipping, or a phone call giving them a compliment for something they did. Most important, make sure to *listen* when you spend time with your mentors. Remember, it's harder to learn when you're the one talking.

While regular contact with mentors is important, I avoid the formality of declaring a relationship to be a mentorship. I do not ask or tell someone they are one of my mentors. That seems to create a burden of expectations for both parties.

I've had the pleasure of mentoring hundreds of people, both young and old, and I receive great energy from the opportunity and highly recommend this practice to you.

A dear friend and mentor, Doug Coe, leader of the Fellowship, once told me, "Some people come into our lives and quickly go. Some stay for a while and leave footprints on our hearts. And we are never, ever the same." Many of the people in this book are my friends. Looking back, I'm quite sure I wouldn't have become successful without the companionship and wise counsel of mentors, friends, and best friends. Be an active friend.

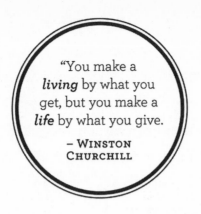

The Power of Service

When I joined the Air Force at age seventeen, I was sent to Texas for basic training. When the drill sergeant requested a volunteer for the position of flag bearer, I raised my hand. At the time, I was five feet, eight inches tall and weighed 114 pounds. The sergeant got right in my face and hollered, "Son, didn't anybody ever tell you 'never volunteer'?" He then selected a bigger kid.

Fortunately, I never learned the lesson. Some of my greatest adventures have been a result of raising my hand to volunteer. Success comes from action. The Gift of Service lies in the fact that by giving of yourself, you get much in return.

Service to others pays tremendous dividends for those who are willing to do more for others, the first (and perhaps most important) of which is that it takes you outside of your own selfishness. I have had the privilege to serve on more than three dozen charitable civic boards, and have participated in countless other service endeavors.

I know about the Power of Mentors and Friends because, as I was coming up in my career, I reached up to a number of people for help, advice, and guidance for both my personal and professional life. I did that by seeking out people who were more successful than I was, in order to understand them better and ultimately become more like them.

As I had the privilege to be mentored by men and women I admired and looked up to, I determined that I wanted to pay it forward by doing the same thing for people who were coming up behind me.

I was always impressed by those individuals who were willing to give freely of their time to someone who couldn't really do anything for them in return. One of the things that I have found to be true in my experience is that most really significant, great people possess this attitude when it comes to giving back to others.

To be a part of your community, you must do your share. Pitch in and get involved with civic and charitable organizations. When you do something for others, it's good for your soul as well as your karma and allows you to spend time with other like-minded people. Whenever you raise your hand, you wind up being asked to do more, and that is great; doing so gives you an opportunity to learn, to impress, to gain skills, and to build new relationships. By doing more than you would otherwise have been able to do, you gain more than you ever would have dreamed.

The best example of the value of learning to be generous with your time and talents is scouting, which is in reality mentoring at its best. Of the twelve men who have walked on the moon, eleven were Boy Scouts. John F. Kennedy, Martin Luther King Jr., Gerald Ford, George W. Bush, and Barack Obama were Boy Scouts. Steven Spielberg, Sam Walton, Jimmy Buffett, Nolan Ryan, and Andy Griffith were too. And the list goes on.

Fostering a culture of volunteerism is fast becoming a part of many successful companies' business plans. My friend Casey Crawford, a former professional football player, has integrated service as a core part of the company he founded with Toby Harris,, Movement Mortgage.

Movement Mortgage encourages employees to volunteer in their communities and to support one another through a "Love Works Fund." The company matches contributions to the employee-assistance fund and has invested several million dollars into the communities where it operates through the Movement Foundation.

More than just writing checks, the Movement Foundation is innovating in how for-profit companies can have a positive impact in their communities. Using its real estate expertise, the company is building Movement Centers, where it brings together various community organizations to serve needy populations under one roof.

This kind of service makes Movement an important part of the communities where it serves, helping the company fulfill its Grand Vision to be a movement of change in industries, corporate cultures, and communities.

As for me, while I have had many opportunities to serve my nation and my community, perhaps the opportunity I am fondest and most proud of came when I met and became friends with a man named Doug Coe, who runs the National Prayer Breakfast. He was extremely generous toward me with his time and guidance.

Coe is the founder of an organization that is now known as the Fellowship, and its fundamental goal from the very beginning was to inspire leadership led by God, empowered by His Spirit. Starting from a small group of men committed to that vision, the Fellowship has been quietly but effectively influencing positive change here in the United States and in more than two hundred countries based on the simple yet powerful belief that the teachings of Jesus Christ have relevance for all people of all faiths and no faith.

Coe once said to me,

Jesus walked the earth and is admired and respected by people from all backgrounds. Different religions view Jesus in different ways, and all acknowledge Him. He lived and died for people regardless of their race, creed, religion, or anything else. His example and teaching were meant for every person. You can speak to anyone about the life and teaching of Jesus, but as soon as you mention Christianity or any other organized religion, you will turn away people of other views.

The Fellowship consists of small, intimate groups working with each other to improve communities, states, and, ultimately, our nation. When explaining the power of these deeply personal groups, Coe once said,

> When it comes to fellowship, size matters: smaller is better. You can worship with a crowd, but you can't "fellowship" with a crowd. To fellowship is to break bread together, pray together, trust together, and help each other talk like Jesus, act like Jesus, think like Jesus, and love like Jesus.
>
> If we do these things, we can learn to love unconditionally, humble ourselves, serve God and not money, give without seeking a return, empower and don't control, show mercy, seek justice and freedom for all people, encourage, spread hope, and believe without doubt. Thence, we will be empowered to see the invisible, believe the incredible, and do the impossible.

Coe eventually asked me to set up a small group of my own in Charlotte, which would come together in faith to fellowship together, eat together, study the teachings of Jesus, and pray together. We have now been meeting together for more than twenty years. Through just this small group in Charlotte, we have been able to serve our community in amazing and incredible ways that have benefited both myself and countless others.

One of the core principles of this group is that we don't talk about the things we do, not for the sake of secrecy, but for the sake of humility. It has been one of the greatest privileges of my life to be able to serve selflessly and sacrificially without the burden of seeking fanfare or recognition, and I am thankful and proud of what our little band has been able to accomplish for the good of our community in the past twenty years.

The following pages feature just a few of my other mentors and friends.

Napoleon Hill (1883–1970)

Author of *Think and Grow Rich*, one of the best-selling books of all time

"What the mind of man can conceive and believe, it can achieve."

In the 1930s, at the height of the Great Depression, Hill studied the success stories of five hundred millionaire contemporaries of his mentor, Andrew Carnegie. He then wrote *Think and Grow Rich*. He observed that, while all of the rags-to-riches stories differed in details, they were the same at the core. Every one of these millionaires kept moving forward, no matter what kind of obstacles they faced. All success begins in the mind. That is why Hill titled his seminal book on success *Think and Grow Rich*. In the author's preface, he alludes to a "secret" in the book. He tells his readers to find that secret within the text because he intentionally didn't make it apparent. Hill states that the "secret" to which he refers is mentioned more than a hundred times. *Think* is repeated throughout the book in every chapter, and I believe it is his secret ingredient necessary for the accomplishment of anything. Note his focus on success:

> The business depression [1929] marked the death of one age, and the birth of another. This changed world requires practical dreamers who can, and will put their dreams into action. . . . We . . . should remember the real leaders of the world always have been men [and women] who harnessed, and put into practical use, the intangible, unseen forces of unborn opportunity. . . . Never has there been a time more favorable to pioneers than the present.
>
> To win the big stakes in this changed world, you must catch the spirit of the great pioneers of the past, whose dreams have given to civilization all that it has of value, the spirit which serves as the life-blood of our own country, your opportunity and mine, to develop and market our talents. . . . "Success requires no apologies, failure permits no alibis." If the thing you wish to do is right, and you believe in it, go ahead and do it! Put your dream across, and never mind what 'they' say if you meet with temporary defeat, for "they," perhaps, do not know that every failure brings with it the seed of an equivalent success.[42]

Hill's book is chock-full of wonderful stories of the many remarkable people he knew and was mentored by over his career.

Dale Carnegie (1888–1955)
Writer, lecturer, and developer
of courses in self-improvement
"Believe that you will
succeed, and you will."

While in college, I adopted Dale Carnegie as a mentor by reading and rereading his seminal work, *How to Win Friends & Influence People*. Written in 1936, the book has sold millions of copies and spawned a training company that still thrives today. Carnegie was the son of James Carnagey, a poor farmer. Perhaps his most successful marketing move was to change the spelling of his last name from Carnagey to Carnegie at a time when Andrew Carnegie was a universally recognized business icon of immense wealth.

Dale Carnegie tapped into the typical person's desire to overcome self-doubt. Like so many other great lessons, his principles are simple but not easy. He said, "First you should not criticize, condemn, or complain. Give honest and sincere appreciation and arouse in the other person an eager want."[43]

He believed that to be liked, you must be genuinely interested in other people. Carnegie encouraged his students to be good listeners, try to make the other person feel important, and respect the other person's opinions.

These are but a few of Dale Carnegie's tools for success. Over the years, countless friends have shared their own stories with me about how his writings changed their lives for the better. Carnegie's work is as relevant today as it was almost eighty years ago.

Dr. Norman Vincent Peale (1898–1993)

Minister and author of *The Power of Positive Thinking*

"The tests of life are not meant to break you, but to make you."

When Norman was a boy, one of his teachers accused him of being "a weak willy-nilly," and he soon realized the teacher's assessment was correct. He saw that he would need to push himself past a deep-rooted inferiority complex and crippling self-doubt. The son of a minister, he decided to follow in his father's footsteps and attended Boston University School of Theology. On a break he returned home and was asked to fill in at a nearby church. He prepared a sermon and showed it to his father who read it and promptly advised him to burn it, saying, "The way to the human heart is through simplicity." He went on to write *The Power of Positive Thinking*, a wonderfully inspiring book, in 1952. It stayed on the *New York Times* best seller list for 186 consecutive weeks and has sold millions of copies since.

Peale's message about believing in yourself changed my way of thinking and living. His words made me realize that if I could not believe in myself, I would never be successful. His saying, "Empty pockets never held anyone back. Only empty heads and empty hearts can do that," was surely written with people like me in mind.

Sir John Marks Templeton (1912–2008)
Billionaire investor, mutual fund pioneer
"Success is a process of continually seeking answers to new questions."

John Templeton was one of the greatest investors of all time. He made his first major investment in 1937 by borrowing money to buy one hundred shares of each stock on the stock exchange selling at one dollar or less per share. His investment quadrupled in four years.

He and his wife set a goal of saving 50 percent of their income to allow Templeton to open his own firm. Launched in 1954, the Templeton Growth Fund became a pioneer in global investments. The fund achieved annualized returns of 15 percent a year until he retired in 1992. Templeton is known for making investment decisions counter to the herd mentality. He has famously said, "Bull markets are born on pessimism, grow on skepticism, mature on optimism, and die on euphoria. The time of maximum pessimism is the best time to buy, and the time of maximum optimism is the best time to sell."[44]

Years ago, I attended a private reception in honor of Sir John. When I arrived, I noticed that he was sitting by himself on one of the couches. The other guests were busy greeting each other. Never one to miss an opportunity, I introduced myself and sat with him. We had a wonderful, wide-ranging conversation and enjoyed each other's company for a half hour or more. One thing he told me was, "I find that if you begin with a prayer, you can think more clearly and make fewer mistakes." He also said, "Keep an open mind. . . . There is always need for more research and more learning. . . . If I had not sought new paths, I would have been unable to attain so many goals."

In the book *Templeton Touch*, the authors state that Sir John was all about discipline and character building.[45] Sir John loved the free-enterprise system. He encouraged those around him to think positively—to be thrifty, especially with the use of time, not letting wasteful thoughts occupy your mind—and to be grateful and generous.

H. Wayne Huizenga (1937–)

Founder of three Fortune 500 companies

"Surround yourself with good people, and you won't fail."

As a young man, when his family's business failed, Huizenga drove a truck and pumped gas after school and on weekends to help out. This came full circle. Starting with a single garbage truck in 1968, he grew Waste Management Inc. into the largest waste-disposal company in the United States. Then Huizenga repeated his business success with Blockbuster Video, creating the country's leading movie-rental chain in its era. He also built and acquired auto dealerships, with which he formed AutoNation, the country's largest automotive dealer and his third successful company. Huizenga created the Floridian Golf Club with two members: himself and his wife, Marti. He then asked a few people he liked or admired to become honorary members at no cost. I was fortunate to become one of the honored few and therefore was able to spend time with Wayne. The only man in history to create three Fortune 500 companies, Huizenga has been a five-time recipient of *Financial World* magazine's CEO of the Year award. Wayne has told me this advice: "Hard work is the secret to success. If you want to accomplish twice as much as the competition, you have to work twice as hard. . . ."

Trammell Crow (1914–2009)

Developer known as
America's largest landlord
"There's as much risk in doing
nothing as in doing something."

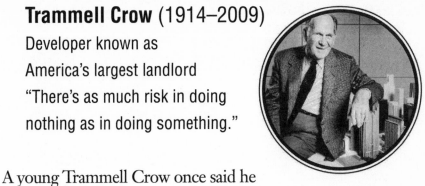

A young Trammell Crow once said he
would never accept an ordinary life. When he graduated from
high school during the Great Depression (1929–1939), jobs
were scarce, so he attended night school to learn typing and
shorthand in order to make himself more marketable. Crow
came to understand the following principle that would become
the guiding force in his life. "It came to me that everything I
would ever do, I'd have to do for myself and by myself. Self-reli-
ance was the most important lesson I've ever learned."

Of his stint in the US Navy, Crow asserted in his acceptance speech as the 1988 Horatio Alger Award winner, "I think
those years were worth a couple of MBA programs to me."

Crow is proof that there is more than one way to earn
an MBA. He had a Grand Vision of great opportunities in
warehousing investments. He began building warehouses
and ultimately built the largest real estate company in the
world. "You can get rich selling real estate," he often said,
"but you can only get wealthy by owning it."

I was a great admirer of Crow early in my career and finally
met with him in 1975 at his offices in Dallas. He believed in
open offices and did not have any walls separating him from

the staff. When I asked about his success, he said, "In your quiet solitude, close your eyes, grit your teeth, clench your fists, and dedicate yourself to achieve . . . and you will."

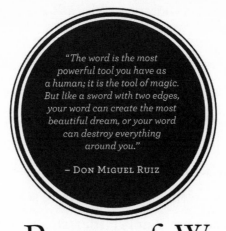

The Power of Words

"Words have a magical power. They can bring either the greatest happiness or deepest despair; they can transfer knowledge from teacher to student. . . . Words are capable of arousing the strongest emotions and prompting all men's actions."

—Sigmund Freud

From childhood, you likely heard, "Sticks and stones can break your bones, but words will never hurt you." This could not be more false. Words have incredible power. The right words can penetrate our hearts and move us to take action, make a change, or question our own beliefs. Think about the historical figure Jesus. His only earthly power was his words and yet today, two thousand years after he walked the earth, his words have power over more than half of the earth's population. More books have been written about Jesus than any other person in history. All of the mainstream religions make positive reference to his teachings. His words, "Do unto others as you would have them do unto you," are some of the best known in every major religion, including Islam.

The wrong words can destroy the lives of millions. A horrific example of the terrible power of words is from Germany, where one man, Adolf Hitler, strictly through the use of words was able to manipulate a nation of intelligent people into a world war and persuade some citizens to commit the most heinous crimes against fellow citizens.

Hitler came to power in a time of economic and social upheaval in the nation of Germany and the rest of the world. He clearly understood the tremendous power of words, stating in his memoir, *Mein Kampf*, "I know that men are won over less by the written than by the spoken word, that every great movement on this earth owes its growth to great orators and not to great writers."

According to Bruce Loebs, a professor specializing in rhetoric at Idaho State University, "[Hitler] learned how to become a charismatic speaker, and people, for whatever reason, became enamored with him. People were most willing to follow him, because he seemed to have the right answers in a time of enormous economic upheaval."[46]

Despite being reportedly a small, awkward man with little talent for face-to-face personal interactions, through the power of his words, Hitler was able to, over the course of more than five thousand speeches, successfully position himself at the head of Germany's most powerful political party, conquer more than a dozen nations, and commit a wide variety of war crimes, including the mass murder of more than twenty million people.

Just as words have a tremendous capacity for evil, they also have an equally large potential for good. It is amazing what a few kind, encouraging words can do in the life of a person.

In his book *The Four Agreements: A Practical Guide to Personal Freedom*, Don Miguel Ruiz says, "Be impeccable with your word. Speak with integrity. Say only what you mean. Avoid using the word to speak against yourself or to gossip about others. Use the power of your word in the direction of truth and love. . . . The word is the most powerful tool you have as a human; it is the tool of magic."

He tells us each word is like a spell, and we can use words like dark magicians, thoughtlessly putting spells on each other. Whenever we hear an opinion and believe it, it becomes part of our belief system. So, say someone calls you stupid or even just implies that you are stupid. Since you are not sure of your own intelligence, you believe him. You have just accepted his opinion of yourself by joining into an agreement with him. Later someone or some event lets you know that you are not stupid. You believe it and make a new agreement. As a result, you no longer feel or act stupid.[47]

This is exactly what happened to me as a young person. I had a stepfather who had only critical things to say to me. More than once he told others or me how little I seemed to know. When I asked once if he would teach me to play the piano since he played well, he let me know that I would never be able to learn to play. That created an agreement in my mind that still exists to this day.

As you read earlier, not until I was forced to join the Air Force and they gave me a battery of tests did I learn that I was not stupid but in fact was intelligent. This knowledge created a new agreement for me, which has served me well the remainder of my life.

Whatever is said about you, don't take it personally. Remember it's not really about you; it's about the speaker. In the case above I took it personally, and believed I was stupid. If you take it personally, you tacitly agree with whatever was said. Even when others insult you directly, it has nothing to do with you. The opinions they give are according to the agreements they have built within their own minds. If people hurl insults or exhibit rude behavior directed toward you, it is in reality due to their own problems and shortcomings. Perhaps they harbor thoughts of jealousy or envy. Maybe they are covetous of your material goods or your closest friend. Maybe they are suffering inside and the only way they can vent the pain is to try to give it to you. Remember, when you are attacked it is never about you.

People will lie to you, and you will also lie to yourself. If someone tells you how wonderful you are, they are not saying it because of you. Don't take anything personally. Even the opinions you have about yourself are not necessarily true.

When you really see other people as they are without taking it personally, you can never be hurt by what they say or do again. If others say one thing, but do another, you must listen to their actions and not their words.

The ability to understand the importance of the precise and careful use of words seems to be critical to success. The use of certain words will help advance your success in life: Use a person's name, as it's the sweetest word he or she can ever hear. Avoid first-person singular pronouns, *I*, *me*, and *my*. Used too often, they make you sound self-centered and self-important. If you use these words regularly, you probably *are* self-centered. Use positive adjectives, such as *terrific*, *great*, *generous*, *wonderful*, *beautiful*, *tremendous*, and *magnificent*. Make your own list of other positive words.

And remember, Will Rogers famously said, "Never miss a good chance to shut up." People have a tendency to talk too much and say too little, especially when feeling nervous. Usually, we're nervous when we're around new people or those who intimidate us.

Many years ago, I was in a critical negotiation with an attorney who represented the company I worked for. In the meeting, I rattled on, talking too much because I was nervous. My attorney leaned over to me and said in a whisper, "Hush, Puppy."

This brief comment said everything. By learning to keep my mouth shut at the appropriate time and simply listen, I was able to discern what was on the minds of the people representing the other side.

Successful people have mastered the art of image-building through words. When you speak with strong intention, your actions take on strong purpose.

When you speak with someone, don't just look at his or her face, but look the person directly in the eye with hard focus and you will be amazed by the direct connection created between you both. Never glance around the person speaking to you, to see who else is nearby. One of the greatest gifts you can give to another is your undivided attention. For some, this is a natural trait, but for most, it must be practiced until it becomes habit.

Some describe this trait as empathy or charisma, but I call it grace and respect for your fellow man. Many times, caring enough to understand what other people believe or want to accomplish can solve an issue that otherwise seems impossible.

Being generous with your words and deeds will take you further in life than being cheap. Plus, you will enjoy the journey far more. Most successful people I know are generous with both words and deeds.

The Rule of Reciprocation

A contemporary version of the Golden Rule is "Treat others as you wish to be treated." In social science, this is known as the Rule of Reciprocation. Professor Manie Spoelstra, director at the International Negotiation Academy in South Africa, states, "The rule of reciprocation, which states that we should attempt to repay in kind what another person has given us, is the most compelling weapon of influence that humanity possess."[48]

If someone passes you in the hall and says hello, you feel compelled to return the greeting. If you don't, you're uncomfortable because you've broken the Rule of Reciprocation. It's one of those invisible, powerful social rules that subtly shape how we behave when someone has given us something. We learn growing up that we're obligated to give back to others in the same form they've given to us.

Phillip Kunz, a sociologist at Brigham Young University, conducted an experiment to see what would happen if he sent Christmas cards to total strangers. He randomly picked six hundred names and sent Christmas greetings. Kunz got more than two hundred replies and commented, "I was surprised by the number of letters that were written, some of them three, four pages long."[49] Some responses even included family photos.

Those preprinted address labels that come in the mail along with letters asking for donations often trigger a real dilemma. You may think you can't send them back because they've got your name on them. But once you've decided to keep the labels, you fall into the jaws of the Rule. You've been given something; how can you, in good conscience, keep it without donating?

The same thing applies to tipping. A recent study produced the following evidence—if a server brings you a check and doesn't include a candy on the tray, you will tip the server whatever you feel is normal. However, if there's a mint on the tray, your tip will go up an average of 3 percent. In addition, if the server looks you in the eye and gives you a second mint while saying the candy is specifically for you, your tip will increase further.[50]

This rule also operates in the medical profession. Robert Cialdini at the University of Arizona states that doctors are more willing to prescribe a specific medication based on gifts, favors, and tips they receive from the pharmaceutical company than those who don't. This is frightening. So, tip more, be generous with compliments, show courtesy, and help others when you get a chance. This Rule of Reciprocity can also have tremendous benefits in your personal and professional life and provide a powerful tool for success. While it has been said that, "nice guys finish last," it has been proven that it is the nice guys who often finish first.

In fact, some research shows that in a long-term collaborative environment like an office, it is always the smart move to be kind and gracious to others, even when they aren't being kind and gracious to you. According to David Rand, the founder of the Human Collaboration Lab at Yale University,

> Usually, colleagues work together for longer than just a few days. People start to realize that if they yield to a coworker one day, he or she will yield to them the next. And even if that specific person doesn't pay the niceness back, someone else might.
>
> According to the theory of indirect reciprocity, others might take notice of your kindliness and form a higher opinion of you in general. Eventually, you might be able to cash in all that good will in the form of a huge favor or pay raise. It's worth noting that this works best if bosses highlight their employees' cooperative behaviors, rather than their sales figures. But the point remains: at work, everyone's playing a long game—one in which the spoils go to the accommodating.[51]

Perhaps even more convincingly, a recent report in the *Harvard Business Review* examined several different studies and concluded that not only can positive, encouraging interactions at work increase productivity and loyalty, but also having a kind boss or coworkers can actually improve your health or the health of your employees. Emma Seppala, writing for the *Harvard Business Review*, says,

An interesting study shows that when leaders are fair to the members of their team, the team members display more citizenship behavior and are more productive, both individually and as a team. Jonathan Haidt at New York University Stern School of Business shows in his research that when leaders are self-sacrificing, their employees experience being moved and inspired.

As a consequence, the employees feel more loyal and committed and are more likely to go out of their way to be helpful and friendly to other employees. Research on "paying it forward" shows that when you work with people who help you, in turn you will be more likely to help others (and not necessarily just those who helped you). Such a culture can even help mitigate stress.[52]

So how can you leverage the Rule of Reciprocity to achieve your goals?

First, remember that it is a two-way street. You can feel obligated by the kindness and generosity of others, but you can also improve your relationships and gain greater influence by doing the same for others.

Second, while it is in your best interest to treat others as you would have them treat you, remember that the Rule of Reciprocity isn't ironclad. If someone expects you to respond to their kindness with a favor that violates your ethical or moral codes, or just wouldn't be good for your business, reputation, personal life, etc., remember that there's not an actual requirement to respond in kind.

The Power of Money

"Money is power, freedom, a cushion, the root of all evil; the sum of blessings."

—Carl Sandburg

Having enough money is a wonderful thing. No matter what Grand Vision you set for your success, unless you plan to become a monk, your path will require the use of money. Having enough frees you to pursue your other goals. It also gives a sense of safety and security. But beware: wealth tends to magnify your underlying character traits rather than change them. It can bring out not only the best in your personality, but the worst, as well. If you're generous by nature, you will be more so when you have money. However, if you're mean-spirited, you may tend to be even more so.

Money is an enabler; it enables you to be more available to focus on your real purpose. It also can enable your compulsive, impulsive, and emotional inner voice to become stronger as your logical, rational voice is pushed aside. Look at the winners of lotteries. The news is full of stories of lottery winners losing it all plus heartache beyond measure. Take the case of a New Jersey lady who won $5.4 million but gambled it all away at Atlantic City. Today she resides in a trailer park. Or a preacher who also worked as a stock boy at a Home Depot to make ends meet. His prayers were seemingly answered when he hit a $31 million jackpot. At first, life was good with the preacher buying a ranch, six other homes, and several new cars. But like many others who win the lottery, he just couldn't say no when people asked for a handout. Later in life he divorced his wife and eventually committed suicide. And then there was the guy who won Pennsylvania's $16 million jackpot. Immediately, one bad thing started happening after another. An ex-girlfriend sued him for a share of the winnings and won; his brother hired a hit man hoping to inherit some winnings, and relatives incessantly bugged him for money. Within a year, he was $1 million in debt and filed for bankruptcy. Now he lives on food stamps and welfare.

The best-kept secret for developing financial independence is to spend less money than you earn—without exception. Start saving money beginning today, even if it's just a dollar, and do it again tomorrow and the next day and then every day. Commit yourself to delayed gratification by putting off impulse purchases so you can keep saving. It's not about how much you start with, but how you finish well. Spend less and invest more is trite but true.

The Magic of Compound Interest

Albert Einstein called compound interest "the greatest mathematical discovery of all time," because it seems to possess magical powers, like turning a penny into $5.3 million. Perhaps you have heard the following question: "Would you rather have a) $10,000 a day for thirty days, or b) Begin with a penny the first day and compound it every day ($0.01–$0.02–$0.04–$0.08–$0.16–$0.32–$0.64–$1.28–$2.56–$5.12 . . .) for thirty days?" If you chose the penny, at the end of thirty days, you would have $5,367,807. If you chose the $10,000 a day payment option, you would have $300,000.

The great part about compound interest is that it will help you achieve financial independence. Simply stated, compound interest means you earn interest on the original amount you save, and then you earn interest on the interest. This phenomenon goes on and on—packing your savings with power and moving you steadily toward your savings goals. This is what I call your Golden Goose. Over time, the results can be dramatic. With the magic of compounding at work, you can predict when you will double your money with the Rule of 72: you simply divide seventy-two by the interest rate you will earn on your investment. For instance, at a constant 6 percent interest rate, your money will double in approximately twelve years (seventy-two divided by six).

Here's a little secret: compound interest is a millionaire's best friend. It's really free money. . . . Starting early is the key.

Purchasing Power

Whether or not you consider yourself a businessperson, every purchase you make is a business transaction, whether it's for a dollar or millions of dollars. Every transaction will fall somewhere on the following transaction scale:

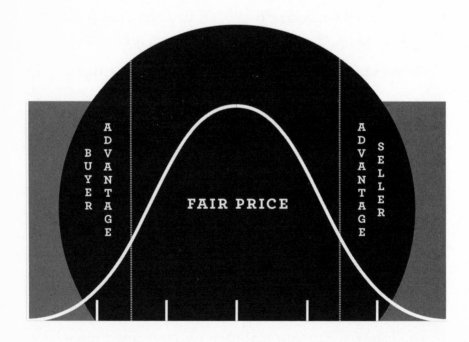

1. The seller receives more than fair market value and the buyer less.

2. The buyer receives more than fair market value and the seller less.

3. Both parties are at equilibrium on value.

All trades take place with one of three results. If you are the buyer, you would like to get a bargain, but if you are the seller, you might like to make an extra profit.

In all transactions, a negotiation will take place. If you take an item to a cashier and hand over the price stated, that's a negotiation in which the seller stated the price and you agreed to the terms. The asking price should only be a starting point, but unless you're willing to become an active consumer and make a counteroffer, it will also be the sale price.

Be intentional in your purchasing habits. Avoid prideful purchases and seek practical purchases. It is not your job to impress the salesman or make their day. Impulsive action is the enemy of value and wealth accumulation. To avoid overpaying, do your research. Most knowledge is now available at your fingertips through online research. The other important traits necessary to achieve value for your money are patience and persistence.

When the price of something offends your sense of reasonableness, you're probably right and should avoid the purchase. After all, only you know how valuable the purchase is to you.

Here's an example: My eyeglass frame broke, so I took it to a national chain that sells frames and lenses. The clerk quoted over three hundred dollars to replace the frame. This offended my sense of reasonableness, so I went on the Internet and looked up the exact eyeglass frame. It cost me twenty-nine dollars online, including shipping. This trip to the Internet saved me a few hundred dollars, and my new knowledge will save me more over the coming years.

Due to being curious by nature, I later tried to find out why the price of eyeglasses ranges from ten dollars at the drugstore to hundreds, even thousands of dollars in national eyeglass chain stores. I discovered that a little-known Italian company, Luxottica, controls approximately 80 percent of the distribution chain for eyewear. Therefore, this company has nearly a monopoly on the eyeglass market. With little to no competition, the company gets to set the price for maximum profit.

While this is certainly a great way for the company to make a lot of money, it was not an advantageous situation for me, the consumer. I would be better off buying the stock of the company rather than their eyeglasses.

As a consumer, cautious skepticism ought to be your default mode; otherwise, you could wind up paying far too much for a range of goods and services, which will ultimately keep you from investing in the things you really care about.

It is always a good thing to determine the actual cost to produce a good or service. It is a huge boon to consumers to be able to avoid dependence on local providers and instead exercise their financial wisdom to find the lowest cost available on the global market. Use my three-way test: Is this something I really need or just want? Is the item or service priced based on a fair profit or an exorbitant profit like the eyeglass frames example? Is this purchase going to be an investment or something that will lose its value over time?

Never think of anything you purchase as an "investment" unless you're almost certain it could appreciate in value under reasonable circumstances. If it doesn't pass this test, it's a consumer item that loses value over time. Many sellers try to create the impression of "fair value" at a high level and then give you a "special deal," which is either at or above true fair value. Car dealers, as well as department and jewelry stores, are famous for this strategy. However, when you find a highly motivated seller, you have the best chance of buying in the buyer advantage area of the chart. If you can determine the seller's motivation, you then have the upper hand in the negotiation.

There are plenty of motivators for people to sell something below its fair market value. For example,

- The sellers are disposing of the remaining contents from their grandparents' house after having removed all of the things they want to keep.

- A shop owner quits the business and wants to move on as quickly as possible.

- A family is moving and wants to reduce the load they are taking with them. Usually family members decided they don't want whatever they are selling and are eager to get rid of it.

- A company goes bankrupt and its inventory is sold by the trustee at bargain prices.

Most consumers give little thought to most purchases. Your job as a careful consumer utilizing the Power of Money is to be thoughtful with your valuable resources. You can double your spending power if, on average, you buy everything at half-off. It's simple but true.

I was once teaching a high school class on the economics of buying power and asked the students to each go into the marketplace and buy something of their choice with the objective of getting the best deal on the item. I offered a prize to the student with the best deal. After a week we heard their stories, and I have never seen sixteen-year-olds more excited. Every student was able to get what he or she wanted well below the asking price. Their techniques were different, and the prizewinner reported she had bought her item at no cost! We were amazed when she reported that she scoured the Internet for various coupons and discounts and by combining two different coupons along with a store discount she was given the item she wanted for nothing.

Many people make the mistake of thinking of items such as new cars as investments instead of as purchases.

Unfortunately, this just isn't the case. Most new cars depreciate in value the second they are driven off of the lot.

In short, when you are spending, ask yourself this basic question: "Will what I'm buying likely be worth more or less than what I'm paying for it in five years?" If the answer is more, congratulations! You have just made an investment.

Ultimately, when it comes to financial success, the key thing to avoid is the allure of what I like to call "shiny things." What I mean is that you should avoid the objects that promise shiny newness, whether that's new jewelry, a new car, a new television, new furniture, or anything else. It doesn't even have to be new. A shiny object is anything that catches your eye, but falls outside your budget, depreciates rapidly, and/or fails to serve a purpose outside the immediate gratification of a desire.

In history, the best example I can recall was the unbelievable trade by the Dutch of some beads and other trade goods to the Native Americans for the island of Manhattan in 1626.

According to *USA Today* personal finance columnist Chloe Della Costa, just a few of the common smaller purchases that can create a roadblock to your financial goals can include convenient snacks and drinks, beauty products, new clothes, overpriced hotels, entertainment, apps, the latest technology, cable TV, and gym memberships.[53]

These are just a few of the "shiny things" you should consider avoiding. When you look at your own spending habits, do any of those items have a prominent or regular place? Consider eliminating them or finding a more affordable alternative. This is one of the best ways to head down the right path toward financial freedom.

A study from the Journal of Consumer Research in 2013 found that "thinking about acquisition provides momentary happiness boosts to materialistic people, and because they tend to think about acquisition a lot, such thoughts have the potential to provide frequent mood boosts. But the positive emotions associated with (actual) acquisition are short lived. Although materialists still experience positive emotions after making a purchase, these emotions are less intense than before they actually acquire a product."

In short, contrary to what most people think, just wanting that shiny new object was more satisfying than actually getting it.

The author of the study went on to conclude, "Materialists are more likely to overspend and have credit problems, possibly because they believe that acquisitions will increase their happiness and change their lives in meaningful ways. Learning that acquisition is less pleasurable than anticipating a purchase may help them delay purchases until they are better able to afford them."[54]

So remember, it might look attractive now, but when you're trying to build your place in the world from survival to sustainability to prosperity, one of the best ways to achieve your goal is to avoid shiny objects.

Collective Power

I n this book, I've laid out a compelling strategy for discovering and achieving your Grand Vision, whatever it may be. And while all of these Powers are wonderful things to possess and develop, none of them will do any good for you in isolation. Success is the direct result of cultivating each and every one of the Powers I've introduced to you—not one or two, not most of them, but every single one.

With the Power to think for yourself, you can drown out the voices competing for your attention in order to determine your dreams and motivations, and live a life where you are the sole person in control of your goals and choices. Don't just accept the status quo. Be interested in discovering why things are the way they are, and be open to swimming upstream against the popular opinion.

The old adage holds true that some of the most dangerous words in the world are, "That's the way we've always done it." Don't accept everything at face value. Instead, seek excellence by always putting forth the effort to find new and improved ways of conducting and structuring your business, personal, and financial life.

By acknowledging and embracing your Power as a Doer, rather than an Observer or a DK/DC, you can join the 1 percent—those who do things and go places others cannot. Using the Powers you have to develop your mind, you can attain intelligence far beyond what you thought you were capable of and strive for goals others think are out of your reach. And by taking the time and energy to understand what makes you who you are, what characteristics make up your personality, you can better understand both your own strengths and weaknesses and the motivations and irritations of others, which are keys to success in any field.

With the Power of Vision, you begin not only to understand what your goals are, but attain these goals far beyond your wildest dreams. By establishing a Grand Vision and setting benchmark goals, you can make each day full and meaningful, and achieve successes that may even surprise you with their scale. Having well-developed goals can literally make you jump out of bed in the morning with energy you may not understand because you aim to get on with your passion.

The amazing thing about vision is that it provides the framework for all of your Powers. Just as a river needs a channel, your Powers need guidance and direction toward a goal, and your Grand Vision is the primary provider of that structure. Avoid spending time in a situation without goals, and instead always be pursuing your next Grand Vision.

With the Power of Knowledge, you can overcome almost any shortcoming. When it comes to self-knowledge, this means knowing your strengths and weaknesses, your passions and desires. The Power of Knowledge also means practical knowledge of your field, hobby, etc. And always remember this truth: knowledge breeds more knowledge. As you grow in knowledge, that knowledge will compound, making it easier not only to retain more knowledge, but also to hold on more effectively and recall more efficiently the things you already know.

Remember that faith is the belief that there are supernatural powers that surpass all human understanding and that strongly influence the fate of us human beings.

The Power of Persistence might be the most important Power in this book. Where you come up short in any other Power, persistence can almost always make up for it. This Power goes hand-in-hand with willpower, which is the ability to do the right thing at all times, even when it's unpleasant or unpopular.

Both are essential to success. With persistence and willpower, there is no limit to what you can accomplish. In the pursuit of any and every goal, the road will get rough, and something in yourself or those around you will try to tell you to stop. Only through willpower can you overcome the desire to quit, whether that means running another mile, doing the right thing, or continuing to pursue a new vocational dream despite setbacks.

With the Power of Hard Focus in your arsenal, you can call up tunnel vision (the good kind) at will to drown out distractions and accomplish what needs to get done. By concentrating with laser focus on the task at hand, you can ignore competing voices and interests, see your objective more clearly, and accomplish things you hadn't thought possible.

In the short term, hard focus means cultivating the ability to crowd out those competing voices for an hour or so a day. In the long term, it means the ability to single-mindedly pursue a goal over the span of months or years in order to see it to completion. Both kinds of hard focus are crucial to your success.

The Power of Mentors and Friends allows you to utilize and serve in your community. It becomes a sphere of influence, both for your own good and the good of other people. Seek out mentors, those who are ahead of you on the path of life, and gain wisdom and insight from those who have gone before. You don't have to accomplish your goals all on your own. You can, in many ways, build toward your dream on the shoulders of those who have gone before you, both living and dead.

Seek out quality friends, and remember the rule of attraction: like attracts like. Because quality people attract other quality people, strive both to associate yourself with those you want to be like and will make you better, but strive equally hard to avoid company that will accomplish the opposite.

Seek opportunities to serve, rather than passively waiting to be asked. Perhaps one the most fulfilling human experiences is the selfless act of giving your time and resources to others. It's been proven time and time again that one of the most important steps on the path to success and satisfaction is to do unto others as you would have them do unto you.

The Power of Words has tremendous potential for good or evil. Words can cause irreparable harm or tremendous good. Words have a beautiful capacity to give life, energy, and positivity to others. Strive to speak positively into the lives of others by encouraging and uplifting them, but also strive to associate with those who will do the same for you. When you surround yourself with people who speak positive things into your life, it's hard not to believe you can accomplish anything, and that's half the battle.

Last, but certainly not least, the Power of Money is enabling and gives you the freedom both to serve others and accomplish your own personal goals. Money is the only Power I've talked about that most people don't start out with. That's why it's so important to work hard at cultivating financial well-being constantly.

Through rational thinking, the magic elixir of compound interest, and the self-discipline to avoid those "shiny things" and empty purchases, I firmly believe anyone can achieve financial health. Why is this so important? Because the enabling Power of Money is the key to a sense of security, the freedom to serve your community in unique and valuable ways, and the fuel that every person needs to achieve their life goals. No matter what your dream is, chances are it's going to require some financial fuel in the tank, and it's always best to start preparing to chase your dreams sooner rather than later.

When all of these Powers are combined, you have the makings of a remarkable journey ahead of you. Don't be discouraged if you don't get every one of these Powers right the first time around, and remember that your mistakes are often more valuable than your successes. Embrace the lessons of failure, remember to stay the course in the midst of success, and never stop striving to get even better at exercising your personal Powers.

That leads me to one last thought I would like to leave you with. Over the years, I have been introduced repeatedly as a "self-made man," but I will share with you that it is just not true. In fact, I think very few people are truly in the category of self-made.

My success was the product of the compilation of wisdom shared with me from uncountable sources. Mentors have given their advice and counsel generously. Failure has taught me about success. Reading great works from history has opened doors to ideas and thoughts from long ago. Friends, as well as enemies, have proven the value of persistence. My faith in a greater Power who rules supreme has been the strong foundation that gives guidance and grace when I simply listen. You are not here alone in this world. Always remember to utilize the resources *outside* yourself alongside the Powers *within*. It is the humility and willingness to accept the wisdom and input of others, even when you might not agree, that will provide the stepping-stones to success.

I hope the lessons for success you have read here will inspire you to take advantage of the opportunities you discover, to achieve success as you define it. You have read about ordinary people who, through the Powers described in this book, have become extraordinarily successful.

They have become famous writers, great inventors, successful actors, industry pioneers, creative innovators, exceptional political leaders, nerds who changed the world, and much more. They have each used their God-given gifts to enhance the world. But all were born just like you and me. They learned to walk and talk like everyone else, by trying and failing and trying again, and again.

They all failed many times but never gave up. Remember, your last option is to give up—and you should save it. It's only through hard work and commitment to getting better every single day that you can achieve goals far beyond what anyone thought possible. So get out there, get to work, and start using the Powers you have been blessed with to achieve your goals every day. I'll see you out there!

Make a Difference—Do Good—Have Fun—and
Never Retire

Acknowledgments

This book stands on the shoulders of so many great people throughout history who made a difference in their time. Their legacies live on for those curious enough or brave enough to seek them out.

It is not a coincidence that the two greatest books on achieving success (*How to Win Friends & Influence People*, by Dale Carnegie, 1936, and *Think and Grow Rich*, by Napoleon Hill, 1937) were written in the midst of the Great Depression, a time when people were humbled and seeking survival with a distant hope for success. Both of these classics are still in print nearly eighty years later.

I am eternally grateful to my wife, Joan, for her encouragement and strong belief in me. My personal assistant, Myra Heafner, has helped me write and edit all of my books. Joan and I refer to Myra as my "office wife" with great affection.

Several people agreed to be "special readers" to provide feedback and ideas for improvement. I am truly grateful to my great friends Melinda Bates, Dr. Tony Zeiss, Frank Martin, Art Ringwald, Willy Stewart, Ambassador Ed Elson, Pulitzer Prize–winning author Mark Ethridge and his son Mark Ethridge, editor Taylor Batten, Larry Polsky, Casey Crawford, Toby Harris, Shia Zhu and her son Leif, and Tom Pollan.

Reading List

As a Man Thinketh, by James Allen, first published as a literary essay in 1902. (Free online: http://www.gutenberg.org/ebooks/4507)

Big Magic: Creative Living Beyond Fear, by Elizabeth Gilbert.

Build Your Own Ladder: 4 Secrets to Making Your Career Dreams Come True, by Tony Zeiss.

Focus: The Hidden Driver of Excellence, by Daniel Goleman.

How to Create Your Own Luck: The "You Never Know" Approach to Networking, Taking Chances, and Opening Yourself to Opportunity, by Susan RoAne.

How to Win Friends & Influence People, by Dale Carnegie.

Love Works: Seven Timeless Principles for Effective Leaders, by Joel Manby.

Mindset: The New Psychology of Success, by Carol Dweck.

One Book for Life Success: Transform Yourself for Peak Performance, by Venu Somineni.

Sacred Contracts: Awakening Your Divine Potential, by Caroline Myss.

See You at the Top: 25th Anniversary Edition, by Zig Ziglar.

The Greatest Salesman in the World, by Og Mandino.

The Million Dollar Toolbox: A Blueprint for Transforming Your Life & Your Career with Powerful Communication Skills, by Ty Boyd.

The One Minute Manager, by Ken Blanchard and Spencer Johnson.

The Power of Positive Thinking, by Norman Vincent Peale.

The 7 Habits of Highly Effective People: Powerful Lessons in Personal Change, by Stephen Covey.

The Slight Edge: Secret to a Successful Life, by Jeff Olson.

The Willpower Instinct: How Self-Control Works, Why It Matters, and What You Can Do to Get More of It, by Kelly McGonigal.

Think and Grow Rich, by Napoleon Hill.

Unstoppable: 45 Powerful Stories of Perseverance and Triumph from People Just Like You, by Cynthia Kersey.

Notes

1. Charles Murray, *Human Accomplishment: The Pursuit of Excellence in the Arts and Sciences, 800 B.C. to 1950* (New York: HarperCollins, 2003).

2. Mike Gaddis, *Legend's Legacy: The Hand at Our Shoulder* (Columbia, SC: Sporting Classics, 2009).

3. "Steve Jobs' 2005 Stanford Commencement Address: 'Your Time Is Limited, So Don't Waste It Living Someone Else's Life,'" *Huffington Post*, last modified December 5, 2011, http://www.huffingtonpost.com/2011/10/05/steve-jobs-stanford-commencement-address_n_997301.html.

4. "George Shinn," *Horatio Alger Association*, http://www.horatioalger.org.

5. Ilya Somin, "Political Ignorance around the World," *The Washington Post*, last modified November 3, 2014, http://www.washingtonpost.com/news/volokh-conspiracy/wp/2014/11/03/political-ignorance-around-the-world/.

6. Devin Dwyer, "United States of Ignorants? Americans Don't Know Constitution, Surveys Find," *ABC NEWS*, last modified March 24, 2011, http://abcnews.go.com/Politics/tea-party-enthusiasm-surveys-find-ignorance-us-constitution/story?id=13206667.

7. "Brain Basics: Know Your Brain," *National Institute of Neurological Disorders and Stroke*, last modified April 17, 2015, http://www.ninds.nih.gov/disorders/brain_basics/know_your_brain.htm.

8. Elizabeth Gilbert, *Big Magic: Creative Living Beyond Fear* (New York: Riverhead, 2015).

9. Dan Hurley, *Smarter: The New Science of Building Brain Power* (New York: Penguin, 2013).

10. Edward de Bono, *The de Bono Group*, http://www.debonogroup.com/edward_debono.php.

11. Robert Sanders, "Intense Prep for Law School Admission Test Alters Brain Structure," *Berkeley News*, August 22, 2012, http://news.berkeley.edu/2012/08/22/intense-prep-for-law-school-admissions-test-alters-brain-structure/.

12. Kendra Cherry, *The Everything Psychology Book*, 2nd ed. (Avon, MA: Adams Media, 2010).

13. Daniel Goleman, *Emotional Intelligence: Why It Can Matter More Than IQ* (New York: Bantam Dell, 1995).

14. Daniel Goleman, "What Makes a Leader," *Harvard Business Review*, last modified January 2004, https://hbr.org/2004/01/what-makes-a-leader.

15. "MBTI® Basics," *The Myers and Briggs Foundation*, http://www.myersbriggs.org/my-mbti-personality-type/mbti-basics/.

16. Jacquelyn Smith, "The Personality Types that Make the Most and Least Amount of Money," *Business Insider*, last modified February 20, 2015, http://www.businessinsider.com/the-personality-types-that-earn-the-most-and-least-money-2015-2.

17. "The Keirsey Temperament Sorter," *Keirsey.com*, http://www.keirsey.com/aboutkts2.aspx.

18. Bruce Charlton, *Psychiatry and the Human Condition* (Abingdon, Oxfordshire: Radcliffe Medical Press, 2000).

19. "Free Learning Styles Inventory, Including Graphical Results," *Learning-Styles-Online.com*, http://www.learning-styles-online.com/inventory/.

20. Darold Treffert, "Tony DeBlois: A Prodigious Musical Savant," *Wisconsin Medical Society*, https://www.wisconsinmedicalsociety.org/professional/savant-syndrome/profiles-and-videos/profiles/tony-deblois-a-prodigious-musical-savant/; see also, "Tony DeBlois," *TonyDeBlois.com*, http://www.tonydeblois.com/.

21. "Science of Daydreaming," *Dartmouth Undergraduate Journal of Science*, last modified February 3, 2011, http://dujs.dartmouth.edu/fall-2010/science-of-daydreaming#.Vf2v3tJViko.

22. Jonah Lehrer, "Daydream Achiever," Life of the Mind, *Boston.com*, last modified August 31, 2008, http://www.boston.com/bostonglobe/ideas/articles/2008/08/31/daydream_achiever/.

23. "The Security Council," *United Nations*, http://www.un.org/en/sc/.

24. "Bill Gates," *Biography.com*, http://www.biography.com/people/bill-gates-9307520.

25. Andrew Khouri and Samantha Masunaga, "Tesla's Elon Musk and His Big Ideas: A Brief History," *LATimes.com*, last modified May 1, 2015, http://www.latimes.com/la-fi-hy-elon-musk-big-ideas-story-so-far-20150501-htmlstory.html.

26. "Forbes 400," *Forbes.com*, http://www.forbes.com/forbes-400/list/#tab:overall.

27. Mark McCormack, *What They Don't Teach You at Harvard Business School* (New York: Bantam Books, 1986).

28. Michael LeBoeuf, *Working Smart: How to Accomplish More in Half the Time* (New York: Warner Books, 1979).

29. Napoleon Hill, *Think and Grow Rich* (Meriden, CT: The Ralston Society, 1937), 31.

30. Derek Sivers, "How to Start a Movement," TED. com, https://www.ted.com/talks/derek_sivers_how_to_start_a_movement?language=en.

31. Daniel Willingham, "How Knowledge Helps," *AFT*, 2006, http://www.aft.org/periodical/american-educator/spring-2006/how-knowledge-helps.

32. Carol Dweck, *Mindset: The New Psychology of Success* (New York: Ballantine Books, 2006).

33. Mike Fitzgerald, "Education Opinion: How the Information Revolution Gives Education the Chance to Be Centre-stage," *The Independent*, last modified August 29, 1996, http://www.independent.co.uk/news/education/education-news/education-opinion-how-the-information-revolution-gives-education-the-chance-to-be-centrestage-1311971.html.

34. Dale Carnegie, *How to Win Friends & Influence People* (New York: Simon & Schuster, 1936).

35. Justin Sachs, *The Power of Persistence* (Carlsbad, CA: Motivational Press, 2009).

36. "Lack of Willpower May Be Obstacle to Improving Personal Health and Finances," *American Psychological Association*, 2012, http://www.apa.org/news/press/releases/2012/02/willpower.aspx.

37. Napoleon Hill, *Think and Grow Rich* (Meriden, CT: The Ralston Society, 1937).

38. J. K. Rowling, "The Fringe Benefits of Failure, and the Importance of Imagination," *Harvard* magazine, last modified June 6, 2008, http://harvardmagazine.com/2008/06/the-fringe-benefits-failure-the-importance-imagination.

39. James Dyson, *Against the Odds: An Autobiography* (New York: Texere, 2003).

40. Mark Cuban, *How to Win at the Sport of Business* (New York: Division Books, 2011).

41. Malcolm Gladwell, *Outliers: The Story of Success* (New York: Little, Brown and Company, 2008).

42. Napoleon Hill, *Think and Grow Rich* (Meriden, CT: The Ralston Society, 1937).

43. Dale Carnegie, *How to Win Friends & Influence People* (New York: Simon & Schuster, 1936).

44. Evan Sparks, "John Templeton," *Philanthropy Roundtable*, http://www.philanthropyroundtable. org/almanac/hall_of_fame/john_m._templeton.

45. William Proctor, *The Templeton Touch* (West Conschohocken, PA: Templeton Press, 2012).

46. Bruce Loeb, "Hitler's Rhetorical Theory," *A New Journal of Rhetorical Studies*, http://relevantrhetoric.com.

47. Don Miguel Ruiz, *The Four Agreements: A Practical Guide to Personal Freedom* (San Rafael, CA: Amber-Allen Publishing, 2012).

48. Alix Spiegel, "Give and Take: How the Rule of Reciprocation Binds Us," *NPR*, http://www.npr.org/sections/health-shots/2012/11/26/165570502/give-and-take-how-the-rule-of-reciprocation-binds-us.

49. Ibid.

50. Reed Fisher, Michael Lynn, Bruce Rind, and David Strohmetz, "Sweetening the Till: The Use of Candy to Increase Restaurant Tipping," *Journal of Applied Psychology* 32, no. 2 (2002): 300–309.

51. Alix Spiegel, "Give and Take: How the Rule of Reciprocation Binds Us," *NPR*, http://www.npr.org/sections/health-shots/

2012/11/26/165570502/give-and-take-how-the-rule-of-reciprocation-binds-us.

52. Emma Seppala, "The Hard Data on Being a Nice Boss," *Harvard Business Review*, last modified November 24, 2014, https://hbr.org/2014/11/the-hard-data-on-being-a-nice-boss.

53. Chloe Della Costa, "Unnecessary Purchases That Eat Up Your Budget," The Cheat Sheet, *USA Today*, last modified March 7, 2015, http://www.usatoday.com/story/money/personal finance/2015/03/07/cheat-sheet-unnecessary-purchases/24507707/.

54. Marsha Richins, "When Wanting Is Better Than Having: Materialism, Transformation Expectations, and Product-Evoked Emotions in the Purchase Process," *Journal of Consumer Research* 40, no. 1 (2013): 1–18.